EEC POLICY TOWARDS EASTERN EUROPE

EEC policy towards Eastern Europe

Edited by
IEUAN G. JOHN
*Woodrow Wilson Professor
of International Politics,
University College of
Wales, Aberystwyth*

SAXON HOUSE | LEXINGTON BOOKS

©Ieuan G. John, 1975.
All rights reserved. No part of this publication may be reproduced, stored in a retrieval system, or transmitted in any form or by any means, electronic, mechanical, photo-copying, recording, or otherwise without the prior permission of D. C. Heath Ltd.

Published by
SAXON HOUSE, D. C. Heath Ltd.
Westmead, Farnborough, Hants., England.

Jointly with
LEXINGTON BOOKS, D. C. Heath & Co.
Lexington, Mass. USA

Robert Manning Strozier Library

MAR   3   1976

Tallahassee, Florida

ISBN 0 347 01093 8

Printed in Great Britain by Robert MacLehose and Company Limited
Printers to the University of Glasgow

Contents

List of contributors

Inis L. Claude, Jr. is Edward R. Stettinius Professor of Government and Foreign Affairs at the University of Virginia, USA.

John C. Garnett is Senior Lecturer in International Politics (Strategic Studies) at the University College of Wales, Aberystwyth.

Frans A. M. Alting von Geusau is Professor of the Law of International Organisations at Tilburg University, The Netherlands, and Director of the John F. Kennedy Institute, Centre for International Studies.

Pierre Hassner is Director of Research at the Fondation Nationale des Sciences Politiques, Paris, and Professor of Politics at the Johns Hopkins University Center, Bologna.

Johan Jørgen Holst is Director of Research at the Norwegian Institute of International Affairs, Oslo.

Ieuan G. John is Woodrow Wilson Professor and Head of the Department of International Politics at the University College of Wales, Aberystwyth.

John Pinder is Director of Political and Economic Planning, London.

Crispin C. Tickell, MVO, is Head of the Western Organisations Department at the Foreign and Commonwealth Office.

Preface

This book is primarily based upon a series of papers by a number of British and European scholars, some of which were presented to a conference held at Gregynog Hall, a residential centre of the University of Wales, 8–11 October 1973.

This conference was the contribution of the Department of International Politics to the centenary celebrations of the University College of Wales, Aberystwyth. The theme of the conference 'To what extent can the enlarged European Community have a common Ostpolitik?' emerged from discussions between the late Woodrow Wilson Professor of International Politics at Aberystwyth, Trefor E. Evans, the editor and other members of the Department of International Politics, and James Cable of the Foreign and Commonwealth Office. But the theme, although it was by no means the first to be suggested or debated, developed in the context of the events of the preceding three years: the initiatives of the Federal Chancellor Willy Brandt, culminating in the successive treaties with the Soviet Union and Poland, and the *Grundvertrag* with the German Democratic Republic; the enlargement of the European Community; and its search for an 'identity' in world politics. During the early part of 1973 it seemed appropriate to speculate on the implications of the expansion from six to nine members for the external relations of the Community and especially its relations with Eastern Europe. That the theme had relevance and significance for the future and merited serious study was apparent.

The organisers of the conference were fortunate in being able to assemble a number of distinguished scholars and men of affairs, including Professors Richard Rosecrance and Geoffrey Goodwin, Dr Karl Birnbaum of the Swedish Institute of International Affairs, Lords Trevelyan, Gladwyn and Chalfont, the Rt Hon Goronwy Roberts, MP, Julian Critchley, MP, and Wyn Roberts, MP, and members of the Foreign and Commonwealth Office and of the French, German, and Italian Embassies in London.

The funds required to enable the conference to be organised were generously provided by the University College of Wales. Valuable assistance was given in various ways by the President of the College, Sir Ben Bowen Thomas, the Principal, Sir Goronwy Daniel, and the Registrar,

Mr T. A. Owen, and by Mr James Cable of the Foreign and Commonwealth Office. The editor also gratefully acknowledges Macmillan's
consent to reproduce parts of Mr John Garnett's chapter in 'The Defence
of Western Europe'. This is the appropriate place to put on record a
tribute to my predecessor, the late Professor Trefor E. Evans, who
contributed so much to the success of the conference and ultimately this
book. His continued and sustained interest ensured the success of the
enterprise. I am also much indebted to all my colleagues in the
International Politics Department for their advice and encouragement, and
in particular John Garnett and Michael Clarke. To Mrs Marian Weston who
coped so patiently and efficiently with the task of deciphering his
corrections and typing the manuscript, and to Miss Dilwen Williams who
assisted in typing one of the chapters, the editor owes a special debt of
gratitude.

Ieuan G. John
University College of Wales,
Aberystwyth
January 1975

1 The Enlarged Community in a Changing International Environment

Inis L. CLAUDE, Jr.

The emphasis of this chapter falls on the subject matter suggested by the word 'environment'. I shall be mainly concerned to discuss not the newly enlarged European Community itself, but the global setting within which it must develop and function, and the enveloping world that defines the problems and possibilities to which the Community must respond if it is to flourish.

Environment is currently a fashionable word among scholars and ought perhaps for that reason to be regarded as a rather dangerous one; the more readily we use a word, the less inclined we are to define it with care and restrict it to its proper usage. Technically, environment refers to that which surrounds the object under consideration, something separate from it but presumably related to it. Commentators on international organisations frequently find it difficult to distinguish those entities from their environments — to establish a clear distinction between the self and the periphery, between the elements that should be regarded as within and those that should be regarded as *around* the organisation in question. The difficulty is most acute when one considers such a quasi-universal body as the United Nations, in which case the decision as to what to relegate to the environmental category may be quite arbitrary. It is less severe when one deals with an organisation of limited membership like the European Community, for it seems logical to include all non-member states in that category.

Nonetheless, one must question the justification for treating the nine states of the Community as a unit detached from the rest of the world, even with the intent of exploring that unit's relationship with the rest. At the least, we must keep firmly in mind the facts that the Community is an integral part of the world, not a foreign body embedded within it, that each of its members is a part of the environment of every other member, and that the Community itself is a part of the environment of the rest of the world. These facts combine to make the Community a part of its own

1

environment, paradoxical as that may seem. The world that affects the Community is the whole world, the world that is as it is partly because it contains the Community — not a world conceived abstractly as the whole minus the Community. Thinking in this vein, I propose to loosen the fetters of the notion of environment sufficiently to permit consideration of 'the world of which the Community is a part' rather than of 'the world apart from the Community'.

The proposition that the world has changed, is changing, and will continue to change strikes us as self-evident. We, members of a generation that is conscious of, and expects change, need no advice about taking change into account. The problem is not whether but how to do this; awareness of the phenomenon does not guarantee accurate assessment of its meaning and significance. I suspect that we stand in greater danger of exaggerating than of underestimating the impact of change, for change is more conspicuous than continuity, just as murder is more newsworthy than acts of friendship. Change proceeds unevenly across the world, and its consequences for international relations may be attributable less to the novelty of what is introduced than to the torque effect, the 'twisting out of joint', that results from its differential impact upon various states and regions. We must remember that change is a collective word for changes that are frequently in conflict with each other — so that the world, in our era of exceptional instability, finds itself 'riding off in all directions at once'. We cannot with certainty distinguish secular trends from ephemeral fluctuations, or predict which changes will triumph in the competition for shaping the future. I shall abstain from any ambitious venture into futurology; there are perils enough in attempting to analyse the significance of changes already in evidence and thereby to develop a picture of the world as it seems to have become and still to be becoming. That is the relatively modest enterprise to which this chapter is devoted.

The emergence of multipolarity

The most sweeping generalisation to be made is that the world is developing a multipolar structure. It is customary to designate at least four states as major determinants of developments in the contemporary international system: the USA, the Soviet Union, China, and Japan. We can postulate a pentagonal structure if we assume that Western Europe, through the European Community, is becoming a meaningful unit within the larger system. The Community's emergence as a fifth major power is a possibility, not an accomplished fact or an inevitable development. The territories and populations embraced by the Community constitute one of the most important centres of power. Western Europe as a region, a collection of states, has global significance whether or not it attains the degree of political unity that would entitle us to speak of it in the singular as a world power. It could take its place as a member of a five-power élite, whose shifting patterns of competition and collaboration can be expected to have decisive influence upon the entire system. In a sense, Western Europe and China share a provisional status in this group; if the former's claim to membership rests on the expectation rather than the achievement of political selfhood, that of the latter rests upon the potentiality rather than the actuality of its development of effective power.

Regardless of the precise way in which the roster of major powers shapes up, the primary implication of the proposition concerning multipolarity retains its validity; the analysis of international politics in terms of a cold war between two superpowers is becoming, or has become, obsolete. This is not to deny the continuing significance of the superiority of the USA and the Soviet Union in military striking power; in the strict thermonuclear sense, bipolarity still prevails. Neither is it to suggest that rivalry and mistrust have been banished from relationships between the two superpowers, or that their antagonistic blocs have been jettisoned. The bipolar struggle has not been abandoned, but it is clearly being limited, muted, and subjected to the moderating influence of rational calculation. It has become more and more appropriate to speak of 'the balance of prudence' instead of 'the balance of terror'.

The central point to be derived from the multipolar trend is that the world's preoccupation with the East—West cold war has sharply diminished. It no longer appears necessary or sensible for every state to define its position with primary reference to the Soviet—American dichotomy, whether as an adherent to one of the blocs or as a devotee of non-alignment. The Soviet—American conflict has become one among many actual and potential conflicts, still important but deprived of its virtual monopoly of international attention.

Hence, the old list of choices for Western Europe has become out of date. Should Western Europe serve as junior partner to the USA in the East—West struggle? Should it aspire to equal partnership, balancing the USA in an Atlantic Community? Should it develop as a Third Force, holding the balance between Eastern and Western blocs? Should it seek to stand aloof from the cold war, claiming a neutralist position? Western Europe no longer regards itself as confined within this range of choice. As it contemplates the possibility of increasing unification within the Community framework, it feels free — indeed, obliged — to ask the question: How should Western Europe play its independent role as one of the several most powerful entities on the international scene?

This emergence of a new range of choice for Western Europe stems from several factors. First, it derives from internal developments. The region has been the postwar scene of an economic and political miracle. Belying the pessimists of the 1930s who insisted that European civilisation would be irretrievably shattered by another war comparable to that of 1914–1918, Western Europe has achieved a most impressive reconstruction and re-invigoration. We must be careful not to exaggerate the degree of its emancipation from vulnerability and dependence, but Western Europe has clearly reestablished itself as an autonomous centre of power in the world. A closely related factor is the moderation of Soviet policy. The sense of being besieged by an expansive Soviet Union has steadily diminished in Western Europe; the combination of increasing strength and decreasing threat has contributed to the expansion of the region's freedom of action. This process has been supported by the dampening of Soviet–American antagonisms. In the early postwar period, Western Europe's insecurity derived from its being not only a potential target of Soviet advance but also a contested area between the giants, a possible battleground for their struggle. As various forms of 'limited adversary' relationship have succeeded the earlier conflicts between the Soviet Union and the USA, Western Europe has tended to gain relief both from the danger of Soviet incursion and from the peril of being caught in the tangles of Soviet–American competition. It is arguable whether the cold war situation was best described as one in which the USA committed itself to intervention on behalf of Western Europe in the latter's difficulties with the Soviet Union, or one in which the United States insisted upon Western Europe's involvement in its own difficulties with the Soviet Union. There is probably some truth in both versions; I suspect that Western Europeans have gradually shifted from the former to the latter interpretation, and this shift may reflect the changing reality of the situation. In any case, the lessening of the acuteness of both sets of difficulty has helped to set Western Europe free to define its international role.

Finally, Western Europe's emancipation from the necessity of defining its position in terms of the Soviet–American division has been promoted by the tendency of the USA to reduce its commitment to active international leadership. Questions about the appropriate degree and manner of attachment to the USA diminish in importance as the latter become less available for attachment. This point is so fundamental that I shall treat it not only as a factor in the broadening of the European range of choice but also as a change in the international picture, equal in impact to the emergence of multipolarity.

4

The decline of American leadership

The word 'less' provides the key to the characterisation of recent trends in the USA's definition of its global role. That country is moving, and promises or threatens to move further, towards being less powerful, less dominant and domineering, less assertive and intrusive, less protective and generous, less vigilant and steady, less willing to take risks, use force, or expend resources. It appears to be less clear than it has recently purported to be about where its interests lie and what is required to safeguard them, and decidedly less inclined to take a broad view of its interests.

Above all, the USA exhibits a shrinking willingness and ability to make and honour commitments. This makes for a drastic alteration of the part that it has played in international relations since World War II. Before that conflict, the leading European powers threatened by Nazi attack were deeply concerned with the question of whether they could persuade the USA to align itself with them clearly enough, firmly enough, and soon enough to avert disaster. After 1945, the questioning was largely reversed; Americans came to ask whether the states of Western Europe could be depended upon to maintain a firm alliance with the USA, to develop effective military forces, to share the burdens of collective defence, to fend off subversion, and to resist neutralist temptations. Since the late 1960s we have seen a reversion to something rather like the prewar situation. It is again Europe's turn to worry about the commitment and the steadfastness of the USA. The issue now is not so much the 'Finlandisation' of Europe as the 're-Americanisation' of the USA.

This is to suggest that the style of performance adopted by the USA after World War II was so atypical, so deviant from national tradition, as to deserve to be considered un-American. It represented a conscious break with the past, a deliberate transformation of policy. What is now at issue is whether history will record it as an aberration or a revolution, an ephemeral shift or a secular change. The implication of present tendencies supports the former interpretation; the USA gives the impression of returning to form, of reviving its traditional aversion to definite commitments and formal alliances.

That aversion has been supported by two rather distinct brands of rationalisation. The earlier brand, which may with some justification be called the Washingtonian, emphasised the weakness and the isolation of the USA with respect to the European centre of world politics. American aloofness from commitment and entanglement was inspired by consciousness of internal disunity, diplomatic inexperience, and military inferiority. The spectre of satellitism convinced the Founding Fathers that their

5

fledgeling state could not afford involvement with powerful allies. Moreover, such involvement appeared to be as unnecessary as it threatened to be dangerous; capitalising on its moated position, the USA found that its limited interests in the European sector were fortuitously served by British policy better than they might be by its own exertions as an active member of the European system. The Washingtonian aversion to alliances reflected a realistic approach to world politics, shrewdly self-interested and based upon accurate appraisal of America's position in the international configuration of power.

This basis for rejection of alliance was supplemented and largely superseded in the twentieth century by the Wilsonian aversion, which may be represented as an idealistic rather than a realistic brand of thought. President Wilson regarded competitive alliances as central elements of the balance of power system to which he attributed the international evils of war and imperialism. The USA was no longer too weak to participate in alliances; it was, so Wilson hoped, too good, too wise, too constructive to do so. At the least, the USA should refrain from immoral involvement in the sordid business of power politics, thereby preventing itself from contributing to global disorder and injustice. At the most, the USA should oppose the nefarious and disastrous alliance system as well as abstaining from involvement in it.

Wilson conceived the League of Nations as an alternative to the alliance system, and envisaged the USA as a leading member of the new and better system. While his enthusiasm for injecting the country into a collective security system did not carry the day, his objection to alliances as contributors to international anarchy was by no means out of line with prevailing American thought and sentiment. Many Americans who opposed membership in the League did so on the ground that such membership too closely resembled participation in an alliance. The domestic defeat of Wilson's project must be attributed in large measure to his failure to convince the American people that in joining the League they would be acting in conformity with, rather than in violation of, their conviction that alliances were sources of discord in international relations. Wilson shared this view of alliances, but he ran foul of it. Whereas the Washingtonian rejection of alliances was based on considerations of national security, the Wilsonian version was motivated by concern for international order. Washington thought in terms of staying out of wars; Wilson thought in terms of preventing them. Washington's mood was one of prudent realism; Wilson's was one of constructive idealism.

In the aftermath of World War II, American aversion to participation in alliances largely disappeared, as was indicated by the development of an elaborate network of alignments centred upon, and fostered by, the USA. It would be a mistake, however, to interpret this as an indication of a radical switch towards affirmative endorsement of the alliance concept by Americans. The essence of the matter was that the country emerged from the War with a new consensus to the effect that it must clearly and firmly commit itself to an active role in building and maintaining world order. The ideologically preferred role was that of leadership in operating an institutionalised scheme for order, somewhat resembling that which Wilson had sought to create. This preference was manifested in the American initiative to form the United Nations and in the decision to join that organisation. The Wilsonian conviction that formation of alliances would be a retrograde step, impeding the success of the organisational experiment and increasing the danger of war, retained a powerful hold. It was only after it came to be widely recognised that the United Nations could not serve as the agent of anything approximating a genuine collective security system, and after the Soviet Union came to be generally regarded as a power threatening world peace and order, that Americans began to define the new role of their country in terms of leadership in a system of alliances rather than in the United Nations. NATO succeeded the UN as the primary symbol of the transformation of American foreign policy.

Whereas Wilson had conceived collective security as a substitute for alliances, alliances now became a substitute for an unattainable collective security system. Involvement in alliances was a second choice for the USA, a concession to perceived necessity. The USA was powerful; the Washingtonian caution against being manipulated and exploited by superior allies could be set aside. The Soviet Union appeared to treat the USA as the major target of its animosity; the Washingtonian assurance that a moated country could safely hold aloof, leaving others the task of managing events in the international arena to which it related only in a peripheral way, no longer applied. The cause was just and the enterprise constructive; under the circumstances, alignment seemed a means to enhance the prospects for a stable and decent world order, exempt from Wilsonian strictures concerning the nefarious effects of alliances. In short, the USA moved from reluctant acceptance of the necessity of alliances to insistent proclamation of their virtue, overcoming its traditional aversion and becoming the chief advocate and architect of a 'free world' system of alignments. The American people convinced themselves that Washington, seeing the necessity, would not object, and that Wilson, recognising the virtue of the move, would not disapprove.

The recent reaction against alliance commitments in the USA has been occasioned and accompanied by the development of a doctrine that combines revived elements of the Washingtonian and Wilsonian critiques with enough that is new to justify the assertion that a third version of American anti-alliance doctrine is in the making. The Washingtonian emphasis upon the country's weakness as a source of danger in alliance has been supplanted by the proposition that the USA is too strong, particularly with respect to new weapons that do not require foreign bases, to need allies. There is a distinct Washingtonian flavour, however, in the contention that the web of commitments spun by the USA in the cold war era entails the acceptance of duties, risks, and costs that cannot be justified by reference to the American national interest. The Founding Fathers would certainly recognise, and might endorse, the claim that their country has imprudently entangled itself in areas outside its proper sphere of concern. Wilson, insisting upon the reality of global interdependence and the indivisibility of peace, would not agree that this extension of the zone of American concern is unnecessary and undesirable, but he might sympathise with another of the major themes of the emergent doctrine: the indictment of American alliance policy on moral grounds.

The revival of Wilsonian moral aversion to alliances is evident in the contention that the USA, by adopting the role of bloc leader, has demeaned itself and betrayed its ideals. It has, so the argument runs, become merely another great power engaged in the traditionally sordid game of power politics — employing the tactics of the big bully, shoring up injustice in the name of maintaining law and order, sleeping with nasty ideological bedfellows, and acting to perpetuate and exacerbate rivalry, antagonism and confrontation. The evils attributed to the USA's performance as kingpin of an alliance system include arbitrary unilateralism, abusive interventionism, reckless militarism — in short, imperialism. Wilson might or might not concur with this evaluation of the postwar record, but he would not in any case find suspicion of alliance connections on moral grounds alien to his manner of thinking.

In addition to these traditional elements, the new anti-alliance doctrine includes heavy emphasis on the theme that commitments to other countries tend to permit and encourage distortion of American constitutional arrangements and political traditions. The President exploits them as bases for the expansion of executive discretion, purporting to find in them the justification for taking actions without the consent of Congress and even in opposition to the popular will. The conventional objection to commitments as impairments of national sovereignty is essentially reversed by this argument. Here, the objection is that the executive branch of government is emboldened to claim and enabled to assert a degree of authority for positive action in foreign affairs that exceeds what the Constitution provides or what sound democratic principles permit. The current movement in the USA to redefine and reassert legislative controls over the conduct of foreign policy stems from a reaction against the alleged use of alliance commitments as instruments for expansion of executive freedom of decision and action. In short, the claim is made that involvement in alliances has tainted the domestic political and constitutional morality as well as the international morality of the USA. The Vietnam War is a case in point; note that its American critics denounced it as domestically unconstitutional and as internationally illegal and immoral — and came to regard the international commitment to which it was related as the root of these evils.

Underneath all this, one sees an emergent bias towards inactivity. Wisdom and virtue consist in *not* doing, on the international scene, what one need not and should not do. The postwar emphasis on bearing responsibility should give way to emphasis on exercising restraint. The USA's contribution to international relations should no longer be defined in terms of 'what we can be reliably expected to do', but in terms of 'what we can be expected to refrain from doing'.

This fundamental shift in attitudes is reflected in alterations of both the realist and idealist creeds. Realism, stressing the doctrine of national interest, seemed earlier to advise American statesmen to 'do what the national interest requires'; more recently, its advice has taken a negative turn: 'do *not* act *unless* the national interest so requires'. Circumspection has replaced resolution as its watchword. Idealism, stressing the goal of peace, has similarly switched from preoccupation with what the USA should do to concern about what it should abstain from doing. Innocence has replaced responsibility as the standard of performance, and pacifism has tended to become identified with passivity.

The realist critique of American foreign policy stresses the theme of overextension; we have tried to do more than was necessary, more than we could afford, more than we could undertake successfully, and more than our share. It develops the image of the overburdened, underappreciated, and underassisted policeman who ought to insist on being relieved and being permitted to concentrate upon problems closer to his own direct concerns. The idealist critique pictures the USA as an overweening imperialist; we have intruded and dominated too much, asserted arrogant pretensions, and thrown our weight around while pretending to bear the weight of the world's burdens. From this point of view, the USA deserves not to be relieved but to be deposed, and it should be pressed not so much to stop trying to do what is unnecessary and impossible as to stop doing what is unconscionable. Whether the advice is to engage in nationally self-interested retraction or in internationally oriented repentance, the purport is the same: the USA owes it to itself, or to the world, or to both, to be less active in the international arena.

This mood, in both its forms, is intimately connected with the emerging American attitude towards commitments. It should be understood that the commitments under attack are those which require, seem to promise, or may provide the President with an excuse for the active involvement of the USA in situations outside its borders. Commitments of a negative sort — not to intervene, or not to act without multilateral authorisation — remain sacrosanct. Thus Senator J. W. Fulbright equally deplored American violation of the commitment not to intervene in the Dominican Republic in 1965 and fulfilment of the commitment to protect South Vietnam; the thread of consistency in his argument was provided by his preference for American aloofness from both situations.[1] Abstention in accordance with commitments if possible; abstention in violation of commitments if necessary — such is the theme.

The same shift of mood is manifested in the urge to subject the President to more stringent congressional and popular control in the conduct of foreign affairs. Clearly, there are important and legitimate legal and constitutional issues involved in this matter. Equally clearly, the central issue has to do with policy preferences, not legal doctrines. After World War II, predominant opinion in the USA focused on the question 'How can we overcome the obstacles to presidential leadership, so that the USA can act effectively and reliably in world affairs?' Currently, the focal question is 'How can we circumscribe the President's authority, to prevent the USA from acting unwisely and wickedly in world affairs?' One does not often hear a senator, a journalist, or even a professor challenging the authority of the President to do something of which the speaker approves. It is equally unusual for a proponent of an active foreign policy, entailing high costs and risks, to advocate expansion of the legislative role in the management of foreign affairs. Such advocacy, for good reason, has normally been the province of those who wish to restrict American commitment and engagement in world affairs. The present case conforms to that norm.

The reader may suspect, from my manner of presentation, that I do not share or sympathise with the change of mood under discussion. That surmise is correct. I am more disturbed than reassured by this trend. Though I am aware that the postwar performance of the USA has been exempt neither from mistakes nor from abuses, I believe that, on balance, it has served the nation and the world well, and I do not see an adequate or acceptable successor to an abdicating USA, waiting to assume the position of international leadership. Careful reappraisal of American policy is in order; wholesale abandonment of position under the impact of an ideology of withdrawal and self-castigation is not. The present mood seems to me more conducive to the latter than to the former. Those who criticise the existing pattern of American commitments and the evolved structure of executive authority are not, in most instances, intent on the indiscriminate destruction of these targets — though they may, by creating and unleashing strong popular forces, destroy more than they intend. Current pressures may be successfully resisted or accommodated, and they may abate. I do not mean to assert that the USA is inexorably set on anything resembling total withdrawal from its international role; one cannot know how far this trend may carry.

That 'one cannot know' is precisely the point that must be understood and taken into account. In earlier times, the USA jealously guarded its right to be unpredictable, treating that as the essence of sovereignty. Today it has lost its capacity to be predictable. It does not so much assert sovereignty as exhibit indecisiveness — uncertainty of capacity to sustain a difficult, costly and morally uncomfortable role, and confusion of judgement and will. For the next few years at least, the world in which the European Community must operate will be one profoundly affected by general uncertainty about the extent to which American involvement and leadership will diminish.

The rise of the South

The reduction of the USA's prominence in the emerging international system is matched by the rising significance of the states commonly referred to as lesser developed countries or as components of the Third World, but which I prefer to designate collectively as the South. Many of these are new states. They are largely non-European and ex-colonial, and are characterised by poverty and what we used to call 'backwardness'. They cluster at the opposite end of the scale from the states that enjoy the rank of Great Power. The problems, needs, demands, and attitudes of the South figure with ever-increasing prominence in contemporary international relations.

A major aspect of the South's growing significance is its status as the locale of actual and potential trouble spots, as distinguished from a collection of trouble makers. This is to emphasise the dangers to which these states are exposed, rather than those that they pose; it is to focus on

11

the problems that they present to the world not because of their policy but because of their predicament. Not their strength but their weakness matters most to the world. Economic, social, political, and administrative inadequacies tend to foster conditions of turbulence and instability that render such states vulnerable to the competitive intrusions of outside powers. Their incapacities make them likely to serve as targets of subversion, objects of rivalry and battlegrounds upon which external forces contend. They tend to exacerbate international relations less by what they threaten to do than by what they tempt others to do — by their victimisation rather than their villainy. The postwar record affords ample evidence of the disturbing effect brought about by the incorporation in the international system of an unusual number of states characterised by marginal or uncertain viability. Learning to cope with the unsettling consequences of the excessive proliferation of new and flimsy states is an urgent task for today's statesmen.

The South's importance for international relations is by no means exhausted by the above analysis. The drive for termination of the colonial system and conferment of sovereign status upon its former components has been fuelled in large part by indignant reaction to the imposed voicelessness and passivity of the peoples who were subjected to that system, and they have not achieved their new status in order to remain silent and submissive. Rejoicing in their newly gained access to the world's microphones, they have become assertive and demanding, clamorous and strident, in presenting their case. The international air is filled with their assertions of need, their claims of right, their definition of justice, and their version of the proper ordering of the world's agenda. They have made the completion of decolonisation, the elimination of pro-white racialism, the abolition of economic arrangements redolent of the colonial era, and the provision of economic assistance central issues of world politics. They demand preferential treatment in compensation for the effects of the adverse discrimination that they recall with bitterness. Their voices, loud and insistent, will not be stilled.

In politics as in economics, it is not mere demand but effective demand that matters; the assertion of claim is less important than capacity for pressing one's claim. Ability to make one's voice heard does not in itself guarantee attention, but must be supplemented by ability to compel consideration. This requisite of effective political demand is being acquired in ever-increasing measure by the South. Membership in the various international organisations that complement the traditional institutions of the global system gives these states votes as well as voices, and provides them with many other and more significant opportunities for influencing the course of events. The states of the South have proved adept at exploiting the instrumental value of multilateral agencies. Not the least of their achievements is their success in setting the ideological tone of the United Nations and its affiliated agencies — a success that perhaps owes less to the volume of their voice than to its correspondence with the still, small voice of the Western political conscience.

The reaction of the West to having its own most cherished principles thrown in its teeth has varied from sullen acknowledgement that it cannot afford to oppose those principles to sympathetic support of the Southern cause. The East, whether from genuine commitment to principles enshrined in its own ideology or from interest in the discomfiture of the West, has presented itself as an enthusiastic ideological ally of the South. For both East and West, considerations of principle and of cold war tactics have combined, in proportions at which the analyst can only speculate, to enable the South to acquire ideological dominance in today's multilateral forums.

The capacity of the South to make its demands effective is not, of course, limited to — or accurately defined by — what it can do in and with international organisations. Members of this group of states, singly and in various combinations, have an increasing array of means, in the circumstances of the present competitive and interdependent world, to ensure that other states not only hear but listen and respond to their claims. They can exploit the advantages of position and the assets of natural resources.[2]

They are in a position to extort as well as to exhort, to rely on terrorist tactics as well as on appeals to conscience. Intimidation and subversion have become two-way streets. In the traditional calculus of power politics, the underdeveloped South appears to be a negligible factor, but in the revised calculus of contemporary international politics, the rebellious South constitutes a force that we would be unwise to discount. The militant revisionism of the South is clearly a major feature of the world in which the European Community must function.

The temper of our times

Having sketched the broad outlines of the world in which the European Community is enmeshed, characterising it as a multipolar system in which the significance of the USA is declining and that of the South is rising, I turn now to more explicit treatment of prevailing attitudes, biases, and moods. If the preceding analysis might be termed geopolitical, this one

13

can be described as psychopolitical, and its subject matter — the dominant modes of thinking and feeling, the temper of our times — is basic to our understanding of the contemporary international system and its prospects.

No feature of today's psychopolitical mood is more prominent than the widespread bias against the strong, the rich, and the established, whether in the domestic or in the international setting. The legitimacy of authority and the propriety of upholding the *status quo* are under strong attack.

Internationally, this mood entails the placing of Great Powers at the wrong end of a double standard and the virtually automatic criticism of their behaviour. They are damned if they do, and damned if they don't; their very status condemns them. They are stereotyped as big bullies, practising the international equivalent of police brutality, and any action that they take in alleged support of international stability is likely to be interpreted as selfish and obstinate maintenance of an oppressive *status quo*. Great Powers are becoming, by ideological definition, ineligible for the application of such adjectives as 'moderate', 'reasonable', and 'responsible'; they are invincibly ruthless, reckless, and wicked. To put it in Gilbertian terms, a Great Power's lot is not a happy one in today's world.

The beneficiary of our most popular international double standard is the underdog, whose ideological position — if not always his geographical one — is southern. The rebel is always right. Justice is to be defined in terms of what the underdog demands, and the achievement of his version of justice is more important than the preservation of peace and order. Ideally, of course, the world should have an effective system of peaceful change, which means the unresisting acceptance of demands for change, excluding any commitment on the part of revisionists to press their claims without violence or similarly to accept negative decisions. Postwar abhorrence of 'appeasement' has been reversed; the new symbol of wickedness and folly is 'confrontation', which refers to the disposition not to surrender to the demands of the ideologically sacrosanct underdog. The beneficiaries of this pro-underdog mentality range from such privileged groups as American university students to the improverished masses of Asia and Africa, though it should be noted that the former feel a compulsion to adopt the guise of pseudo-proletarians or pseudo-peasants in order to justify their inclusion in the underdog category.

The international system is plagued by the existence, and challenged by the insistence, of an enormous number of underdogs who are all too genuine, and who deserve greater sympathy than their more vehement ideological hangers-on are likely to inspire on their behalf. However clearly we may recognise the moral and prudential necessity of responding to their plight, we should not delude ourselves about the psychological ease of entering into a helpful relationship with them. In the international setting, it is blessed neither to give nor to receive; the imprecations to be expected by the generous giver are hardly inferior in quality to those likely to be directed at the stingy abstainer from assistance projects. Certain facts about underdogs must be faced with tolerance and understanding. They bark a great deal, and vociferously. They frequently bite the hand that feeds them. Moreover, they insist that overdogs have a solemn obligation to feed the mouth that bites them. They need help, but are difficult to help; they demand it, fear it, and resent it. Sympathy may supply the essential motive for assistance, but it is demeaning, and conflicts with their most critical demand — the demand for respect. Today's international underdogs resist dependence, but demand dependability. They are inclined to suspect talk about interdependence as camouflage for intrusions upon their independence. It may prove easier for the West to develop a constructive approach to the problems of the South than to develop a comfortable psychopolitical relationship with the states and peoples of that region — today's quintessential underdogs.

I do not mean to present this anti-Great Power mood as the property exclusively or even primarily of peoples outside the Great Powers. Speaking with particular reference to the USA, my own country, I find it very much an internal phenomenon. American opinion has been drastically influenced in recent years, and future American policy must surely be significantly affected, by a deeply critical — even hostile — appraisal of the performance of the USA as a Great Power. The pessimistic view of the American record tends to call forth a profound scepticism as to whether the country can be expected or enabled to perform more acceptably as a Great Power and, indeed, to promote the view that Great Powers as such are incorrigible enemies of justice, of progress, and of any international order worthy of being sustained.

'We have sinned' is the slogan. It was inspired mainly by our involvement in Vietnam, but has been applied retroactively. I have found that many American students, reading Vietnam backwards, find it almost impossible to believe that the USA has ever done anything decent or constructive in international relations, or to conceive that it might do so in the future. In reaction to the abuses of anti-communism, they have developed a vehement anti-anti-communism that leads them to condemn postwar America as an imperialist trouble maker, the instigator of an unnecessary cold war and of wars far from cold, the chief oppressor of helpless and aspiring peoples, and the shrewd and ruthless agent of the prostitution and manipulation of the United Nations. They react with incredulity of any suggestion that the sins of the USA might have been in some measure balanced by service as a key defender of the values of Western civilisation and as a supporter and invigorator of the ideals and activities of the United Nations.

A significant clue to the trend of American political ideology is to be found in the fact that those who employ 'liberalism' as a term of approbation now tend to equate 'liberal' with 'leftist'. They despise McCarthyism, but they have adopted the view of liberalism that they rejected so indignantly and rebutted so successfully when it was advanced by Senator Joseph McCarthy. If today's American radical is not enamoured of liberalism, this is because he believes that it does not conform sufficiently, or that it conformed too belatedly, to the definition given by his ideological *bête noire* McCarthy. The 'left-liberal' position is that, short of the drastic transformation of American society and politics, the USA can escape its career of international iniquity only by incapacitating itself for further wickedness. Self-immobilisation is the recipe for recovery of American respectability put forward by those who view the possession of significant power as an irresistible temptation to indulge in abusive international behaviour.

The USA's postwar performance may or may not deserve the unfavourable evaluation described above; honest men are entitled to disagree in their judgements of the record. It is a fact, however, that a significant sector of the American body politic has developed a sense of guilt that lends moral appeal to the suggestion that Great Power status should be renounced. Many who are deeply concerned with moral responsibility now believe that this entails asking not how to perform the Great Power role but whether to perform it. It is open to question whether any modern society can 'enjoy' Great Power rank; power is more likely to be associated with shame than with glory.

The anti-Great Power bias of our time is closely connected with an emergent pacifism of a peculiar sort. War is sweepingly condemned as having no possible rational or moral justification, and this assertion is seldom qualified by any acknowledgement that a differentiation should be made between attack and defence, between aggression and protection. In point of fact, no one can evaluate a particular war as a single unit, for every war has at least two opposing sides — and if the military activity of one side is considered unjustified there is a strong probability that the response of the other will appear warranted. If A attacks B, the very lack of justification for A's assault provides the justification for B's defensive response. Contemporary pacifism is actually more discriminating than it sounds. Apart from a few absolute pacifists who explicitly reject the principle of violent self-defence, most members of the 'anti-war move-ment' confine their opposition to selected halves of wars. For instance, Americans who vehemently opposed 'the Vietnam War' typically directed their antagonism exclusively against the American–South Vietnamese part of the war; if they believed that the other half of that war made no sense, could not pay, and deserved condemnation, they were remarkably inept in conveying that message.

Today's peculiar pacifism in fact derives its criterion for evaluation of military engagements from the pro-underdog and anti-Great Power ideology. Fighting for a cause that enjoys the endorsement of this ideology is not 'war', the pejorative connotations of that term are reserved for ideologically unsanctified military ventures, including those launched in opposition to approved campaigns. The old question, 'who is the aggressor?' has not been discarded, but the old problem of defining and identifying the aggressor has been easily solved by applying the ideological test: the aggressor is the party whom a right-thinking person would wish to lose the war.

For Americans and others of this persuasion, it is difficult to conceive of a military struggle that might be waged by the USA or, more generally, by the Western powers that would be eligible for approval. This mood is, of course, subject to change, and a clearcut attack upon home territory would doubtless produce a sudden surge of enthusiasm for the concept of legitimate self-defence. In all the contingencies that seem likely to arise in the near future, however, American or Western military response will be handicapped by the prevalence of the sentiment that the establishment's causes are unworthy ones. The domestic force of this sentiment is great enough to cast serious doubt upon the availability of the USA for leadership in any forcible effort to maintain international stability or to resist the undermining of the bases of such order as the world now enjoys. Any rationalisation of a conflict in those terms would engender profound scepticism on the part of a segment of the American public that has shown considerable ability to hinder the carrying out of foreign policies of which it disapproves.

For better or for worse, the USA's contribution to the cause of world order in the next few years seems likely to be in accord with the preferences of those who see the possibility of American moral rehabili-tation in the cultivation of the virtue of innocent restraint and abstention.

One may point out, correctly, that those in the USA and elsewhere in the West who explicitly espouse or accept the ideology of self-flagellation and the prescription of self-immobilisation constitute a relatively small, albeit a powerful, minority. We would do well, however, to confront the fact that the tendencies initiated by this minority are reinforced by the drift of the majority. The general temper that has developed in the West, which must be ranked as a significant element of the psychopolitical environment of the European Community, is marked by an inward-looking tendency, a new privatism. We sense an erosion of commitment to public purpose, a loss of public spirit, a decline of what Walter Lippmann has called 'the public philosophy'. National self-confidence and self-esteem, and the positive allegiance to which those qualities give rise, have been overtaken by disillusionment, weariness, cynicism and apathy. Inspiration and vision are lacking; the West is experiencing a failure of verve, a breakdown of confidence in the validity of its ideals, the worth of its traditions, and the integrity of its institutions.

One may be tempted to attribute this dispirited, disenchanted and disoriented state of the West to the poverty of leadership. Charismatic leadership has recently been in short supply. It is symptomatic of our situation that we now emphasise only the modest demand that our leaders have 'credibility' — and that we sometimes hope in vain for even that minimal and essentially negative quality of leadership. Not since the death of John F. Kennedy has an American President shown any capacity for inducing his nation to believe in itself; his successors, however substantial their achievements, have not stirred the national imagination.

We should be cautious, however, about excessive reliance on the notion that inspired and inspiring leaders might provide the cure for the Western malaise. The weakness of leadership may be the effect as much as the cause of the prevailing mood. Socieities that are in no mood for heroics are unlikely either to choose leaders having heroic qualities or to follow them if they should gain office. It is noteworthy that every postwar American President save Eisenhower has been, in some sense, destroyed in the office — and the fortunate exception was a man whose appeal lay largely in his identification with a relaxation of national effort. A deep aversion to assertive and adventurous leadership is a characteristic of the current American temper. As the case of Henry Kissinger suggests, we are prepared to applaud the performance of a diplomatic virtuoso — but this does not mean that we are willing to accept the discipline of a maestro; a soloist, unlike a conductor, places no heavy demands upon us. It may be closer to the truth to say that we mistrust leadership because we are disinclined to engage in strenuous international activity than to say that we are shifting towards international passivity because we mistrust our current leaders. Though I have emphasised the American case, I think these observations about the availability and the acceptability of leadership have a wider application. This is not a good season for aspiring heroes in the West.

18

The unhappy mood of the West may be, above all, a consequence of the successes of the past quarter century. Our achievements in many fields have been impressive; one could make out a case that the West has displayed, to an exceptional degree, such qualities as vigour, imagination, wisdom, compassion, and generosity. It might seem logical to expect such a record to give rise to sentiments of pride and self-confidence, but it is one of the ironies of life that the reaction to success is often quite the reverse. One is tempted to say that nothing fails like success. It appears that our spiritual malaise is in part traceable to our affluence; we have become fat, lazy, bored and self-centred. We have encouraged the problem of the irrepressible bulge, discovering that the solution of any problem creates at least one new problem. Our progress, far from providing an opportunity for relaxation, has posed the necessity for new and more strenuous effort. Admirable reforms on behalf of the underprivileged, in both domestic and international contexts, have aroused, not soothed, revolutionary impatience. Our present discontents may well be reactions to the failure of our success.

The world that surrounds and includes the European Community presents a stream of problems that runs continuously into the future. The central question for the Community is no longer how it should relate itself to American leadership in tackling those problems, but how it should respond to a developing vacancy in the position of leadership. Europe faces an opportunity and a challenge, not so much to replace the USA as to take the lead in reviving the Western sense of purpose and stimulating a renewed willingness in every sector of the West, the USA included, to accept the costs and the risks entailed by responsible international performance.

Notes

[1] *The Arrogance of Power*, Penguin Books, London 1970, chapters 4 and 5. See especially pp. 95–97.

[2] This chapter was written as a paper and delivered before the Arab states began their vigorous use of the oil weapon, following the Middle Eastern War of 1973 – which provides a striking confirmation of the point.

2 The Changing Structure of Security in Europe

Johan Jørgen HOLST

The complex process of change

The framework of Western security arrangements is changing. We can all recognise the fact that we have moved beyond the postwar era, but the direction in which we are moving remains unclear. The concepts of 'Atlantic partnership' and a 'peace order for Europe' harbour sentiments which are widely shared, but they do not embody much specific guidance for policy making. What is needed is some operational precision in regard to the short and medium term movements.

In periods of transition it is easy to be overwhelmed by the mobility and novelty of the political environment. Vision is sometimes distorted by a disproportional emphasis on that which is new at the expense of continuities with the past. Judgements are sometimes impoverished by impatience and the intrinsic attraction of a desirable future. Predictions are often petrified by implicit assumptions about inexorable progress in desirable directions which ignore the possibility of detours and setbacks. Expectations are at times confused by a propensity to overlook the time distance separating the present from the preferred future. But there are also, of course, the obverse dangers of fossilisation fostered by a tendency to perceive the present through filters moulded by familiar 'realities', or an insistence on the permanence of the established pattern of interstate relations in Europe.

The difficulty of coping with the process of change at the present time stems to a large extent from the simultaneous occurrence of four central processes of change. It is the interaction of these processes and the differentiated rates of change that occur within them which is causing confusion and uncertainty. The processes at work include:

1 The process of normalisation across the East—West division in Europe.
2 The process of integration in Western Europe.
3 The process of formalising relations between the two superpowers.
4 The process of redistribution within the Atlantic Alliance.

B

Security issues and the structure of security arrangements are central to all four processes. The process of normalisation involves modifications in the military infrastructure of the political order in Europe by means of force limitation arrangements. The process of integration in Western Europe following the enlargement of the European Community will focus on the gestation of a European identity which would, over time, have to embrace the realm of defence. The process of formalising the relations between the two superpowers involves a transition from a *de facto* to a contractual arrangement to prevent a nuclear holocaust and alleviate the burdens of nuclear deterrence. The process of redistribution involves a reallocation of responsibility, influence, and burdens between the United States and the states of Western Europe for the common defence.

The structure of peace in Europe

The system of security in Europe is structured around the two alliances, NATO and the Warsaw Pact (WP). Each of the alliances is led by one of the superpowers. The nature of the leadership and the basis for its acceptance are very different. These basic asymmetries are important features of the security system.

The confrontation between the two alliances has been concentrated in the core area of Central Europe. It has been muted in recent years by the explicit recognition of the territorial *status quo*. Competing perspectives and expectations prevail with regard to the evolution of political relations across the lines of sociopolitical and military confrontation. A process of mutual penetration and access is likely to generate new perceptions about the nature of the security problem in Europe. Till now, however, the perceptional evolution that has taken place has not resulted in any reduction in the military confrontation. On the contrary, the Warsaw Pact has taken several measures to augment its military power, possibly in an attempt to obtain extra bargaining counters in the negotiations about force limitation in Europe.

NATO in particular serves the function of linking the three security zones in Europe, i.e. Northern Europe, Central Europe and South Eastern Europe into a coherent and cohesive defence system. It constitutes an institutional expression of the notion that peace in Europe is indivisible. Preferential détente and force limitation arrangements could cause fragmentation and dissolution of the coherent structures.

The security of the European states is closely connected with the stability and configuration of the central balance of deterrence obtaining between the two superpowers. In NATO a perennial problem has been how to arrange for special drawing rights for the countries of Western Europe on the US strategic deterrent forces. The arrangements have involved intensive consultations and joint planning (NDAC/NPG), forward basing of nuclear systems which would link the strategic deterrent to the land battle of a war in Europe, and the stationing of American forces in Western Europe as a guarantee of substantial US involvement in the event of aggression. Britain and France have taken out their special insurance against long term uncertainties with regard to the American nuclear umbrella. Nuclear weapons imply a need for central decision making; there is no way of sharing the actual decision about when and how to use them. For this reason nuclear weapons are a poor cement for community construction. It is feasible, however, to design cooperative systems of planning which will be important in terms of crystallising options and conditioning behaviour and choices when a decision has to be made.

NATO now has to adjust to a situation of codified parity on the level of the Soviet–American central balance. How will it affect the feasibility and credibility of extended deterrence? How will it affect the nuclear shadows which have in the past enveloped the politics of Europe at critical junctures? How will the objective solidarity of the superpowers, forged by the nuclear burden, affect the subjective solidarity upon which the Atlantic partnership should be built? The security of Europe is inextricably linked with the nuclear peace. But how will the political process in Europe be affected by a trend towards nuclear de-emphasis in the postures and operations of the superpowers?

Transatlantic security has rested on the readiness and ability of the United States to commit and support forces for the defence of Western Europe. In recent years we have often observed how important sections of the American political establishment have wanted to reduce the American presence in Europe. There is a feeling that the job has been done, that the cold war is over or waning, that Europeans ought to carry a larger share of the burden, and that priority, in terms of the commitment of money and attention, should be given to the domestic problems of the USA. The alienation and frustration bred by the wars in South East Asia, and the crisis of confidence and institutional strife between Congress and the President, which was exacerbated by Watergate, contribute to the political turmoil and reassessment. The predictability of American decision making and its susceptibility to European influence has been reduced. Europeans have on the whole refused to acknowledge the pressures that operate over the troops issue in Washington. Or they have tended to view American withdrawals as a kind of natural catastrophe which may happen some day, but whose occurence and consequences lie beyond what it is within their power to influence.

From a political point of view it can certainly be argued that the primary task is one of finding a level and form of American engagement in the security arrangements in Europe which can mobilise broad bipartisan support in Washington. A contractual arrangement, which would probably involve some reductions, could stabilise expectations in regard to the American presence and provide a firm basis for East–West negotiations about mutual force limitations. It seems useless to approach the problem from the point of view of equity since there is no way to determine objectively what constitutes an equitable distribution of burdens and costs. It is necessary for the USA to identify the burdens and costs they would like the Europeans to assume. Many figures with regard to the absolute costs as well as the foreign exchange costs associated with the American military presence in Europe have been brandished about in the American debate about the troops in Europe. Serious intra-alliance discussions and negotiations are possible only when there is a concrete proposal or request on the table. Bilateral offset agreements could not provide long term stability. What is needed is some sort of contractual and multilateral agreement about burden sharing in general, and the foreign exchange costs of American troops in particular, which will permit the alliance to approach negotiations with the East in a confident and coherent fashion.

To some extent the possibility of negotiating mutual force reductions with the Warsaw Pact countries has operated as a kind of substitution mechanism. The resolution of problems concerning relations between members of the Western alliance has been postponed or transferred to the level of East–West negotiations. As the negotiations get under way they are likely to acquire a life and purpose of their own. They will impose a heavy load on national bureaucracies which will find it difficult to handle East–West and West–West issues at the same time. The orchestration of the timetables of the various East–West negotiations will generate powerful pressures, which will render difficult a coordination of East–West force reductions and constraints on the one hand, and a restructuring of the NATO posture on the other. East–West negotiations may come to complicate otherwise desirable reconfigurations of the NATO posture, as all existing elements and structures become potential bargaining counters in the negotiations.

Transatlantic security arrangements have also rested on the American command of the Atlantic ocean. The build-up of the Soviet navy has provided Moscow with an important bargaining instrument in a crisis and a serious threat to Western supply lines in a war. The implications of this changed state of affairs are particularly worrying for the states in Northern Europe which are now located behind the Soviet forward defence lines in the North East Atlantic.

Transformation via force limitations

On 30 October 1973 negotiations opened in Vienna on Mutual Reduction of Forces and Armaments and Associated Measures in Central Europe. MURFAAMCE is an impossible acronym so we shall use the shorter MFR, Mutual Force Reductions. There used to be a 'B' in here for Balance, but it was dropped along the way. This was probably all to the good since the voluminous NATO studies on relative force capabilities showed that in this particular comparison of apples and oranges it is really impossible to apply a common denominator of assessment. There are basic asymmetries in the organisation, equipment and doctrine of the WP and NATO forces. Thus the current commitment to the principle of undiminished security conveys rather accurately how the final assessment must be based on subjective evaluations.

It seems likely that any reduction scheme to be negotiated in the first rounds in Vienna will have to conform to a rather simple formula.[1] An equal reduction of Soviet and American forces in the reduction area (Poland, the German Democratic Republic, Czechoslovakia, the Federal Republic of Germany, Holland, Belgium) by 15 per cent may be a reasonable first step. It would imply a reduction of some 30,000 American and 70,000 Soviet troops. More important, perhaps, than the specific percentages is the unit of reduction. Choices in this area will affect the flexibilities with regard to force restructuring. Reductions in the form of major formations, such as divisions, could seriously curtail NATO options regarding the future structure. Thus it might be preferable to think in terms of battalion packages. Furthermore, mutual force reductions may be exploited as a mechanism to bring about restructuring. Thus a change in the teeth-to-tail ratio[2] may be facilitated by NATO's preservation of the option of a preferential reduction in the size of the non-combatant elements. The non-combatant proportion of all NATO divisions amounts to about 40,000, while the adjusted non-combatant component of Soviet divisions is only about 20,000.

It is also possible to envisage trade-off agreements which would involve a preferential reduction in, for example, particularly offensive but unequal elements on both sides. Such an agreement in respect of Soviet tank units has been suggested. This approach may also be applicable to various short range nuclear missile systems. Utilities in this context should in addition be viewed in the context of novel technologies. Thus new anti-tank weapons and area effect weapons may change the threat assessments in connection with Soviet tank capabilities and consequently the price of Western counterparts within a trade-off reduction arrangement.

Another issue relates to the reduction of non-superpower forces. The Western European powers with forces in the reduction area initially took the view that Soviet—American reductions should be accompanied by reductions of other forces in the area. The scale of reductions could be smaller than that which would apply to the Soviet and American forces. The reduction factor could be, for example, half of that which would apply to the forces of the superpowers. Such a formula raises some important political issues, since the refusal of France to participate in any force reduction agreement and the location of Britain outside the reduction area would result in the emergence of internal frontiers within the European Community, separating the areas subject to force reductions from the rest. It could have a rather disintegrating effect on the future consolidation of the Community, particularly as the two major 'outside powers' are also the nuclear powers in Europe. For the European Community the important political issue is that of preserving access to the avenues leading to greater integration. Thus the Nine have resisted Soviet attempts to constrain their options by proposals for national sub-ceilings on military forces in the reduction area, and the erection of barriers against new institutions for defence cooperation. At the same time the European powers in Vienna have been interested in negotiating about the procedural links between the reduction of superpower forces and those of the other participating powers, so as to insure some momentum of the process, and an equality of status and involvement.

There is also the further danger that a sub-regional force reduction formula of the kind referred to above would tend to separate Central Europe from the rest of the European security area. The practice of selective détente and arms regulation could develop into a challenge to the concept of indivisible peace in Europe. The consequences could be particularly unpleasant for the countries in Northern Europe where the links to the general balance in Europe constitute a *sine qua non* for the maintenance of regional restraints and equilibrium. The problem of security fragmentation is increased by potential shadows which may be cast over the countries on the northern and southern flanks of NATO by the continued expansion of Soviet naval operations and capabilities.

Considerable confusion and ambiguity seem to prevail about the purpose of force limitation arrangements. It may be useful to distinguish between objectives which relate to defence policy and those which encompass wider security policy considerations. MFR as a means of solving defence policy problems would put the accent on reducing the scope of peacetime expenditures and force levels and, possibly, on bringing about a reconfiguration of the existing posture. The American approach appears to have been determined largely by such objectives, probably because the institutional pressures in Washington focus on the level of force problem. It is arguable, however, that defence policy objectives 'belong' on the level of negotiations between the Western allies and that transferring the issues to an East–West level cannot but weaken the Western alliance.

Security policy objectives connected with MFR would presumably focus on the role of force problem in Europe, i.e. on how to shorten the political shadows cast by military forces and activities in Europe. Such an orientation results in different priorities from the former. The emphasis will be on regulating and constraining activities rather than on defining a state of affairs. The wider purpose would be to reduce the military factor in the normal flow of politics in Europe. From such a perspective the predominant purpose would not be to save money or reduce manpower levels, but rather to save European politics from the tyranny of military pressure. The focus will be less on limiting capabilities than on reducing their applicability and relevance.

The so-called 'associated measures' or 'constraints' would aim in this direction. They would include 'non-circumvention' arrangements, 'verification' and 'stabilisation' measures. The stabilisation measures could encompass commitments to announce movements into the reduction area or manoeuvres inside it in advance. They could also limit manoeuvres in the reduction area or in specific areas of major security concern, such as national frontier zones. They may involve the exchange of observers during manoeuvres. Non-circumvention measures would be designed to stablise a reduction agreement by regulating the redeployment of forces from the reduction area and the rotation of forces between outside areas and the reduction area. Verification measures may involve surveillance by fixed observation posts, land mobile and air mobile inspection teams as well as high altitude satellite photography.

Such measures need not be restricted to the reduction area. In fact, a strong case can be made for applying the constraints to the whole of Europe and serving the integrating function of upholding the notion of the indivisibility and coherence of the security arrangements in Europe. The constraints could presumably lend operational precision to the principles of interstate behaviour which will be discussed and probably approved by the Conference on Security and Co-operation in Europe. The immediate objective need not be a direct curtailment of the capability to commit military aggression or employ demonstrations of force for purposes of intimidation. It could focus instead on building thresholds against the employment of force and on influencing perceptions and expectations so as to release some political relationships from the military embrace. Here we are referring to tendencies and trends rather than absolute conditions. From such a perspective the value of reducing the Soviet military presence in Eastern Europe would be viewed in terms of how it might influence political perceptions and expectations in Eastern Europe, rather than how it would affect the direct military threat to Western Europe.

Several of the constraints, such as a commitment to announce military manoeuvres and major troop movements in advance, prohibition of manoeuvres in national frontier areas and of troop movements across national frontiers except as part of routine manoeuvres, restrictions on redeployment and reintroduction of forces, etc., would lend substance to the concept of the equality and sovereignty of the states in Europe. That concept is, of course, not sustained solely by juridical contract. Here is an important link with the agenda of the Conference on Security and Cooperation in Europe, CSCE. A beginning may be made in the direction of establishing a network of interstate and intersocietal penetration and dependence. An even tighter web of interdependence will presumably give all the powers involved a stake in the peaceful evolution of the political order in Europe. Thus we may think of the possible agreements from the talks on MFR and those emanating from the CSCE as constituting elements of a total package of short term insurance and long term investments. A special problem in this connection involves the relationship between the so-called confidence building measures, to be negotiated in Geneva during CSCE, and the constraints, or associated measures, which will be discussed during the MFR talks in Vienna. The talks in Vienna will presumably focus on the kinds of constraints which would stabilise a force reduction agreement by incorporating non-circumvention provisions, while the CSCE negotiations would aim at more general regulations. From the point of view of security policy objectives, a greater overlap may become desirable.

The Western defence posture in Europe

NATO's current defence doctrine is outlined in MC 13/3, a Military Committee document defining the strategic doctrine of the Alliance and based on the concept of flexible response. The range of flexibility comprises three basic levels of response: direct defence, deliberate escalation, and general nuclear response. These responses would not necessarily be initiated in succession. The basic concept involves tailoring the response to the scale and scope of the attack. The NATO doctrine, furthermore, embodies the principle of forward defence. This concept is considered to be of primary importance, particularly by the Federal Republic of Germany, but it is vital to other 'frontline' countries such as Norway and Denmark. Forward defence does not imply a requirement for rapid counteroffensives against the territory of the adversary. It assumes that defensive operations should be initiated as early as possible and with a minimum loss of territory.

The defence layout comprises screening and covering units in forward deployment to identify aggression and attempt to canalise it; the main forces which are stationed in the defensive areas; immediate reinforcements such as the two American dual based brigades of the 1st infantry division; and the reinforcements by forces which maintain a lower level of readiness. The relative emphasis in the configuration of the defence posture is different in the various NATO areas. Thus on the Northern flank the screening and covering units as well as the main forces in being are all indigenous forces; the immediate reinforcements are provided by the ACE, but the major external reinforcements would come from the US Marine Amphibious Force (M + 30 days), the UK Mobile Force (M + 10 – 20 days) and the Canadian air/sea transportable combat group (M + 30 days), where M = Mobilisation Day.

There is little need to alter the basic concept of flexible response, but the structure of the forces and options should clearly be under continuous review. There are some obvious weaknesses in the NATO posture. Some are endemic and derive from the geographic asymmetries of the two superpowers as regards territorial proximity. Some are organisational such as the existence of a multiplicity of national logistic systems in NATO. There is also a problem of maldeployment as the American forces are concentrated in Southern Germany while the defence across the major invasion routes in the north German plain is less impressive. And there are other structural deficiencies, for example in air defence.

Due to the possibility of American troop reductions in Europe much attention has recently been focused on the US 7th Army in Germany. It comprises the 5th and 7th Army Corps with headquarters at Frankfurt-am-Main and Stuttgart respectively. The 5th corps includes the 8th infantry division and the 3rd tank division. The 7th Corps comprises the 3rd infantry division and the 1st tank division. The two remaining brigades are dual based. The manpower is stationed in the USA and the equipment is prestocked in Europe as well as in the USA so that in fact there is a double set. Every second year the brigades are airlifted to Europe as part of the so called 'reforger' exercise. The total manpower of the US Army in Europe is about 190,000. In addition there are 130,000 men associated with USAFE and USNAVEUR. It should be observed that the USA has already reduced its forces stationed in Europe from the 1962 peak of 434,000 by about one quarter.

In Central Europe the NATO forces total nearly 24 full divisions comprising 719,000 men and 5,880 battle tanks.[3] The Warsaw Pact figures are 59 divisions, including 28 Soviet divisions, with a total of 925,000 men and 15,550 tanks. The Warsaw Pact forces have been reinforced by some 1,200 T-62 tanks over the last year. The older tanks have not been withdrawn, but only moved on the rear positions. NATO has a small numerical disadvantage in fighter bombers (1200 − 1400) and a much smaller number of interceptors (350 as against 2,100). Long range and payload have had a lower priority in the Warsaw Pact air forces than in NATO, which has maintained a long range deep-strike tactical aircraft capability. The Soviet Union has, however, chosen to build an MRBM force which could in some circumstances perform similar tasks.

Comparisons of the two force postures are difficult and the competing assessments frequently seem tailored to prove points and support preferred options in regard to negotiations and budgets. Several suggestions have been made for restructuring NATO forces so as to increase the number of fighting units with a given input of manpower. It is argued that Soviet forces are designed to peak early in a war and that the NATO posture ought to be tailored more specifically to an anti-blitzkrieg role. The changes in the NATO posture should include changes towards smaller units, higher teeth-to-tail ratios, and a chequerboard in-depth defence. It is contended, furthermore, that the new conventional technology involving precision guided munitions (PGMs), modern area effect weapons, new anti-tank weapons, etc. will provide new options for a plausible defence. Thus the argument is made that by restructuring NATO forces in Europe conventional parity is within reach and that the introduction of several new technologies may produce superiority in defence. The restructuring which would result in reduced standing armies and budgetary expenditures may be accompanied by improved mobilisation capabilities.

It has been suggested that the NATO defence layout may be altered by reassigning missions involving the American forces in Europe and moving them into SACEUR's reserve for rapid commitment to the most vulnerable part of the front in an emergency. The American forces are

30

strong in armour and air mobility. An American air mobile reserve force in the centre could also be used more easily for reinforcement of the flanks, should such reinforcements become urgent. Brigadier Kenneth Hunt of the International Institute for Strategic Studies has outlined an alternative three-layer defence concept based on a mixture of regular and militia units for forward defence, a main defence consisting mainly of heavily armed mobile formations, and a third layer of cadre formations designed to receive local and other reservists as well as some of the reinforcements.

Such reconfigurations of the NATO defence posture should be considered in the context of adjustments to mutual troop reductions, budgetary pressures on military expenditures, the social pressures which are operating on existing conscription systems, and, perhaps most important, the need to design a force posture that is as consistent as possible with a political climate of détente and a sustained momentum of political reconstruction. It would seem of particular importance to identify the kinds of options, in regard to restructuring, which should be upheld and not curtailed by the negotiations about MFR. Constraints on movements of forces, in particular, should not prevent reinforcement exercises of the 'reforger' type; nor the kinds which are practised in North Norway.

The Icelandic government has now concluded a process of reassessment with regard to the American troop presence at Keflavik. From the point of view of North European security a desirable compromise seems to have been found which would permit the American defence force to continue operations from Iceland. Some important changes in the modalities of the airfield operations will be implemented, including the transfer of certain operational tasks to Icelandic civilians and a clearer separation of the military and civilian parts of the airport. The important contribution of the maritime surveillance patrols from Keflavik to the stability of transatlantic and East—West relations has not been generally appreciated. The same applies even more strongly to the importance of the early warning radar capabilities and fighter protection, which constitute a *sine qua non* for the credibility of the North American security guarantee to Northern Europe.

Current NATO doctrine includes 'Provisional Guidelines for the Initial Tactical Defensive Use of Nuclear Weapons'. These will be complemented in due course by another set of guidelines for the follow-on use of nuclear weapons. Much discussion has centred around the proper role of nuclear weapons in the defence of Western Europe. The critical questions have focused on battlefield use and employment in extended areas. Some differences of emphasis prevail between the German and American views, as the former tend to emphasise demonstrative use for purposes of influencing the intentions of the adversary and the latter to focus on how to decide military battles. Nobody prefers early and massive use of nuclear weapons. The USA tends to oppose early use, whereas the Federal Republic of Germany opposes massive use. The reasons for the differences in emphasis are quite obvious.

Most of the tactical nuclear weapons in Central Europe are ground based, including a considerable number of air defence weapons. The rest are included in the NATO strike plans and are primarily air based. The delivery systems include 56 MGM-31A 'Pershing' missiles (range 460 miles), 30 MGM-29A 'Sergeant' missiles (85 miles), and the MGR-1B 'Honest John' free rockets. Sergeant and Honest John will be replaced by the lower yield MGM-52A 'Lance' (75 miles). The nuclear artillery tubes include the M-109 155 mm howitzer which is available only to CENTAG, and the higher yield 8-inch M-110 howitzer which is deployed with units in the NORTHAG area. The nuclear strike aircraft include some 280 F-104G 'Starfighters', 230 F-4 'Phantom IIs', and 25 'Buccaneer' light bombers. The Federal Republic has opposed the prechambering of ADMs as has Norway on the Northern flank.

The present generations of tactical nuclear weapons should, according to some observers, be supplemented and partly replaced by the new generation of 'mininukes' which apparently permit a high measure of deliberate control and target discrimination. It should be noted, however, that any modernisation of the nuclear posture which would imply greater control and calibration could also give rise to fears of a *de facto* decoupling of the US strategic nuclear guarantee to Western Europe, particularly in the context of codified strategic parity. The tactical nuclear weapons in Europe constitute, in the eyes of many observers, a critical link in a continuous chain of options. Some of the tasks of tactical nuclear weapons in the current posture could presumably be transferred to PGMs with high explosives, while others may conceivably be transferred to high accuracy MIRV'ed strategic missiles. Thus the new conventional technology could raise the nuclear threshold, improve the plausibility of a conventional defence option in a certain range of contingencies and permit substantial reductions in the arsenal of so-called tactical nuclear weapons. The force balance in Europe should not be assessed in terms of static comparisons of force assemblies, but rather in terms of the options which either side may want to retain, or, obversely, deny to the adversary. For very good reasons statesmen are going to remain extremely reluctant to transgress the nuclear threshold. They are unlikely to consider weapons which obscure or obliterate the salience of the threshold as very attractive.

In contemplating tactical nuclear warfare scenarios, there is always the problem of retaliation or pre-emption on the part of the adversary who may refuse or be unable to play according to the preferred 'rules'. We shall never be able to fight highly controlled anti-septic nuclear wars with very confident assurance against dirty and disastrous eruptions. But these issues primarily concern relations between the Western countries. Any negotiations about tactical nuclear weapons in Vienna would raise fears of Soviet manipulative diplomacy, and an East—West agreement could freeze the level much beyond what can be sustained by rational analysis.

The SALT premise

The importance of the SALT I agreements probably rests more in the promise for the future than in what was consummated. The initiation of a process of contractual formalisation of the framework and rules of strategic deterrence may herald a new epoch in which the shadows of nuclear holocaust dwindle and the role of nuclear weapons in the normal flow of politics diminishes. But what would be the impact on the alliance guarantees which have been structured around nuclear deterrence? It is impossible to tell, of course, but the invention of nuclear weapons cannot be reversed. The residual uncertainties about their final arbitration will continue to make nuclear deterrence an inevitable and primary feature of the security system in Europe.

The Soviet—American agreement on prevention of nuclear war of 22 June 1973 constitutes another formalisation of a *de facto* recognition of many years, i.e. the shared interest in preventing the outbreak of nuclear war. It involves the application of the principle of abstaining from the use and the threat to use force in a particular context. The agreement reflects the dialectical transition from mutual deterrence to mutual dependence and reassurance. It may come to constitute an added barrier to the first use of nuclear weapons. But the evolution of a formalised nuclear de-emphasis commitment will reflect and register a *de facto* situation rather than constitute a novel departure. Thus a no-first use commitment[4] may come to prevail by implication and general recognition rather than by explicit agreement. But the residual uncertainties will remain.

SALT is still in its infancy. The interim agreement freezing the levels of strategic offensive forces must in a few years' time be replaced by an extended or permanent agreement. The Russians have been working hard to expand their options and close the qualitative gap in regard to MIRV.

Thus four new missiles have been tested: a solid fuel successor to the SS-13, the SS-16, which may provide an option for a mobile configuration deployment, the liquid fuel SS-17 and SS-19 which have been tested with MIRV package methods and finally the follow-on to the large SS-9, the SS-18, which has been tested with a MIRV package of six 1 MT warheads. Moscow has also flight-tested a new extended range SLBM, the SS-N-8, which apparently will be fitted into the twelve or sixteen tubes of the Delta class submarines. The ICBMs have also been tested with cold-boost launching techniques permitting the emplacement of larger missiles in existing silos. The USA is modernising the land based missile force by introducing 550 MIRV'ed 'Minuteman-3's. 31 of the American strategic missile submarines will be retrofitted with MIRV'ed 'Poseidons', and eventually the ten oldest boats of the 41 submarine fleet will be replaced by Trident submarines, according to present plans, towards the end of this decade. The new submarines will each carry 24 Trident I (C-4) 4,000 nautical miles missiles or the larger Trident II (D-5) missile. The USA is developing new precise warheads which will expand strategic options with regard to targeting and firing rates.

Much discussion has focused on the forward based systems, FBS, the strike aircraft which can deliver nuclear weapons to targets on the territories of either of the two superpowers. The current Soviet definition of FBS, which seems designed to exclude the Russian medium bombers, would include only those nuclear capable NATO aircraft that are able to strike targets in the Soviet Union on two-way missions. Thus the American formula for a non-circumvention agreement would apply only to the F-111E squadron in Britain, and possibly to elements of the 16th US Air Force in Spain to the extent that its aircraft are temporarily deployed to forward bases. The Soviet M/IRBM force is so large that marginal as well as very substantial reductions would contribute little to a diminished threat to Western Europe.

The strategic postures of the two superpowers exhibit some rather basic asymmetries which derive from differences in tradition, technology, targets, geography, and commitments. It would seem preferable that a future SALT agreement be structured in terms of agreed limitations of broad aggregates rather than a detailed and symmetrical obligation. The limitations on aggregates could apply to e.g. budgets, throw-weight and number of weapons. The particular mix would be left to each of the parties to decide.

We have come to a dead end in the search for a reasonable doctrine upon which to build a stable balance of nuclear deterrence. The doctrine of 'mutual assured destruction' is not just a viable expression of our best efforts to attain security in the nuclear age. Men of conscience, humanity, and a sense of aesthetics will want to transcend the twisted logic of the present state of affairs.

Deterrence is a psychological variable which cannot be expressed in numbers of dead citizens and percentages of destroyed industry. Strategy has parted with political objectives when the deliberate destruction of civilians becomes a means of dissuading and influencing decision makers who are not invariably sensitive to the needs and wants of those civilians. The divorce is also caused by the calls which are sometimes heard from would-be arms control proponents for massive and prompt retaliation on the basis of incomplete evidence about the objectives and the intentions of the adversary. Responsibile nuclear deterrence cannot be had on the cheap. The technological developments which permit a broader range of discrimination and deliberate control in the exercise of military power constitute in many ways a *sine qua non* for the eventual realignment of strategy, politics, and ethics.

The long term challenge we all confront is to construct a more rational order which is consistent with our political objectives and human compassion. Important steps have been taken in the direction of a peaceful order in Europe. On the level of nuclear deterrence we shall probably have to move away from punitive deterrence and towards active and passive defences. Nuclear weapons produce some of the most intractable existential problems of our time. The deficiency of the current arrangements provides no excuse for continued inattention, complacency, or abdication of responsibility.

Notes

[1] The Vienna talks are still in progress at the time of going to press (March 1975), but no advance has been made towards even a minimal agreement. The Western negotiating position is based on a proposal for a 15 per cent reduction in the US and Soviet forces in the first phase, followed by the fixing of a common ceiling of 700,000 men for the NATO and Warsaw Pact forces in the second phase. The latest Soviet bloc proposal provides for a first stage reduction of 10,000 men in the Soviet and American forces based in Central Europe; this will then be followed six months later by a second stage shared reduction (involving a total of 20,000 men) in the forces of six NATO and Warsaw Pact countries.

[2] Teeth-to-tail refers to the proportion of combat and non-combat

elements in a division, i.e. non-combat units being primarily understood not as units which would not be expected to fight in certain conditions, but as units whose primary function is to support the fighting elements, i.e. through logistic support, communications, signalling units, etc.

[3] If we include France then there are nearly 26 divisions totalling 777,000 men and 6,200 battle tanks.

[4] This refers to the commitment not to resort to the use of nuclear weapons first.

3 The Soviet Response to Western European Integration

Ieuan G. JOHN

My purpose in this chapter is to survey and explore the reasons for the Soviet attitude to the ongoing process of Western European integration (particularly, in its most recent phase, the enlargement of the European Community), within the context of the motives, objectives and strategy of Soviet foreign policy; to attempt both to understand and explain the factors which have led the Soviet leaders to adopt such attitudes, and finally to examine the ways in which they might respond to future trends in the Community. This last task involves an element of speculation more risky in the case of the Soviet Union than for other powers.

Most students of Soviet affairs would appear to agree that ideology is one of the dominant influences on the formulation and conduct of Soviet foreign policy. It provides the Soviet leaders: first, with certain general but significant long range objectives; second, with a 'scientific' system of knowledge which enables them to analyse the international system and identify the 'objective' conditions prevailing during succeeding historical stages and, perhaps less confidently, in the short range phases; and finally, with an overall strategy and operational tactics. The next major factor is the totality of interests of the Soviet Union as a major power, and in the last decade or so as one of the two dominant nuclear superpowers. Perhaps we should include the pride of Soviet leaders in their achievement of this exalted rank, impelling them to expect and strive for substantially greater global influence. In addition there are the constraints imposed on Soviet policy makers by a range of domestic and external pressures, which presumably affect their tactical responses to rapidly changing politics – economic conditions. Clearly Soviet policy is the outcome of a complex interaction between these three and probably additional elements.

Ideology and the formulation and conduct of Soviet foreign policy

If we are to believe the statements of Soviet leaders and other exponents of Marxism–Leninism, ideology continues both to condition their

37

perceptions of the realities of international politics and to determine long range foreign policy goals and strategy. A Soviet author wrote in 1967 that the foreign policy of the working class, of its political parties and of the governments of communist controlled states aims at the revolutionary transformation of the entire existing system of contemporary international relations in conformity with the requirements of objective laws of development. In other words the policy aims at creating favourable international conditions for the liquidation of capitalism and the victory of socialism in all countries.[1] There is little or no evidence to suggest that Soviet leaders have abandoned the view that the world is divided into two camps, which are not the conventional type of rival coalitions or alliances found in the past, but different socio-economic systems. The conflict between them cannot be overcome. Peaceful coexistence is consequently only intended to apply to the period of transition between the erosion of capitalism through its inherent contradictions, and its replacement by a world system of socialism; peaceful coexistence does not mean the acceptance or confirmation of the *status quo*; it is a dynamic form of struggle.

Soviet policy makers armed with the science of Marxism—Leninism are concerned with analysing the processes and the nature of change, and particularly with identifying the point at which quantitative is transformed into qualitative change. The crucial questions to be explored and answered are the character of the present historical period, the relationship between productive economic forces and political processes and institutions – of particular relevance to attitudes towards European integration – and the major trend in the present historical period. It is suggested by some students of Soviet policy making that this process of analysis, identification and evaluation precedes the choice of appropriate policy options.

Long term goals and policies

Current analysis of the prevailing historical phase appears to have confirmed the confidence of the Soviet ruling élite, – grounded in the basic tenets of the ideology – in the inevitable victory of socialism. The long term historical character of the process of transforming the old and capitalist system into the new is stressed: 'the dynamics of the process is measured not within the scale of individual events, but within the framework of specific historical periods . . . having advanced considerably, the forces of socialism and progress are now fighting for the consolidation of their success and for making it irreversible.[2] Recent theoretical articles reflect the extent to which this confidence has been reinforced by the signs of economic and financial instability and social tensions in the industrial countries of the capitalist world in the wake of the energy crisis. This has led to the view that it would be irrational, unnecessary and unjustified to risk a military conflict merely to accelerate the tempo of a process whose outcome was not in doubt. 'The overall ratio of forces in the world' writes one Soviet commentator and theorist, 'is steadfastly changing in favour of socialism — whatever superiority the forces of the new world may achieve in the future over the forces of the old and departing world, the reliance on victory at the cost of the death of millions of people, and the destruction of material values in the flames of war, is alien to the future of socialism.'[3]

Some students of Soviet affairs consider that deliberate recourse to war, while it cannot be excluded, is unlikely anyway, due not merely to the faith of Soviet leaders that time is on their side, but to the present balance of forces. But there is and continues to be debate about the extent to which this caution is influenced by the perceived dangers of all-out nuclear conflict and by their sustained conviction in the inevitable victory of the socialist camp.

However, it is improbable that the Soviet Union will abandon their goals or dispense with the threat of force or employment of their military capability as an instrument of diplomatic pressure and political influence.

However much Marxism—Leninism may influence or even determine Soviet long range goals and strategy or provide Soviet leaders with the Messianic faith that they are borne forward on the tide of history, and with the assurance that the success of their cause is derived from the 'objective' process of economic change, its relevance to the more immediate predicaments they face, and its ability to offer guidance in short range policy decisions is at least open to question. Although they claim that their science provides the basis for analysing micro-foreign policy as well as macro-foreign policy problems, does it do much more than create a framework for the assessment of situations and adoption of rational responses to them? Communist ideology does not offer a detailed guide to action.

Short term goals and policies

What then is its role in the conduct of short range policy, in the choice of tactical options? Soviet policy makers presumably utilise the usual combination of technical skills in collecting information about the external environment, but selection and assessment of the information will be affected by their ideologically motivated and conditioned perceptions of reality. We may ask whether and to what extent they are aware of divergences and contradictions between the external environment and their evaluation of it. Are short range actions taken in response to situations created by external events and forces and then retrospectively rationalised and legitimised in the form of authoritative statements of the ideological position? Or do protracted ideological debates and a definition and, if necessary, reformulation of doctrine precede the choice of policy options? If one accepts the view that one of the important roles of the ideology is to give legitimacy to the Soviet leadership within the Soviet Union and the world communist movement, the second might be more likely to represent what actually takes place. Soviet leaders must always be concerned to justify their actions as not only consistent with but positively required by the principles of Marxism—Leninism. Even if their adherence to part or whole of the communist credo were to weaken or cease to exist, the maintenance and use of the ideology might continue to be necessary to the legitimisation of their political authority. However, there could be cases where events might demand a quick response, with little time to go through the extended process of doctrinal argument. Brzezinski takes a cautious view that Soviet short range moves are only in part a function of the situation as created by outside forces, but adds 'that there are situations to which the Soviets have to respond and about which they have relatively no choice.'[4]

Soviet short range actions cannot be isolated, however, from the same factors which determine their long term commitments and goals. Soviet leaders no doubt face from time to time the need to distinguish between momentary expediency on the one hand and major concessions in ideological principles on the other in the interests of temporary compromises.[5] Such distinctions are thought to be crucial by Soviet leaders. Any derogation of principle would mean a surrender to the ideology of the class enemy and a betrayal of socialism, and as such a qualitative change in long term policy and objectives. Thus any and every shift in short range policy must not impair the fundamental tenets of Marxism—Leninism. However, the Soviet leadership's task is made easier by the control which they exercise over the interpretation, adaptation and textual manipulation of doctrine, as well as by the ambivalences and often conflicting strands of an ideology, inherited from its founder and developed by his Russian mentor, neither of whom could have foreseen all the circumstances which confront their latter-day disciples. Soviet leaders have consequently been able to emphasise differing elements of the doctrine, and creatively adapt its principles to new situations. We need only remind ourselves of the nuances in the interpretation of 'peaceful coexistence', of the different meaning given to the term by the Soviets in propaganda aimed at the non-Soviet world on the one hand, and within the Communist Party on the other hand.

Soviet status and role as a superpower

Confidence and pride in the recently acquired influence and status of a superpower can also be expected to play a major role in the behaviour, policies and general objectives of Soviet leaders. They combine a nationalist faith in the greatness of their country, inherited from Russia's historic past, with a conviction of its unique role as the midwife of the future socialist world society. They have succeeded in completing the final phase of the transformation of their state from a great Eurasian power to a world power, and sole effective interlocutor with the USA. Under their direction the Soviet Union has achieved parity with that country in nuclear deterrent capability and in addition has improved and modernised the weapon systems of its conventional military forces, and established itself as a world naval power. The expansion and deployment of Soviet naval forces may to some extent be influenced by a strong feeling that a state which wishes to be regarded as a world power must possess a global maritime capability.

This accumulation of immense military strength, while it does not ensure foreign policy success or guarantee the immunity of its prestige and political influence from risk, does provide the Soviet Union with the reasonable assurance that its territory is unlikely to be directly and deliberately attacked. One might reckon that this greatly enhanced sense of security in the remainder of the 1970s and in the 1980s would enable them to give greater priority to their domestic problems and needs. If in fact the Soviet Union had become a politically conservative power, satisfied in the main with the *status quo* it might be expected to divert resources from military expansion for these purposes. However it is doubtful whether the Soviet Union is a *status quo* power in any except a territorial sense. Its leaders' perception of its revolutionary role, even if the consummation of the aim to transform the capitalist system is only considered possible in the relatively long term, is likely to mean that the Soviet Union will continue in the foreseeable future to be influenced by the primacy of foreign policy.[6]

41

It would not be surprising if the Soviet leaders should feel that they have a right to be consulted and to exert their influence in the same measure as the leaders of their adversary superpower. But their incentive to expand their range of influence may be reinforced by their recognition of the fact that the maintenance of the Soviet Union's hardwon states as a superpower may require as much effort as its acquisition in the first place.[7] Indeed one of Moscow's preoccupations in the next decade may well be to prevent, or failing that, to delay the entry of potential candidates into the exclusive privileged club of superpowers, an aim which has particular relevance to the Soviet attitude and policy towards the European Community.

Soviet antagonism towards Western European integration, 1948–61

Soviet attitudes and policies towards the European integration process were consistently hostile between 1948 and 1957. In response to the launching of the European Recovery Programme in 1948, the Soviet government and party mounted a propaganda and diplomatic offensive, punctuated by recourse to more overt coercive pressure in the Berlin Blockade. If its reaction to the Schumann Plan was expressed in a lower key, that to the European Defence Community was perhaps naturally more vociferous and sustained; it waged a protracted campaign combining specific threats and vague inducements to the major participants in the negotiations of the EDC treaty. Although it would be an exaggeration to credit the Soviet Union with the exclusive influence in the demise of the project, it may have contributed substantially to the French rejection of the treaty. In March 1957 Moscow addressed diplomatic notes to the governments of the Six, warning them against concluding the Rome Treaty and thus establishing the European Economic Community and Euratom. This remonstrance was accompanied by a proposal to reactivate and strengthen the United Nations Economic Commission for Europe as a framework for closer cooperation between Western and Eastern Europe. The ratification of the Rome Treaty, the creation of the communities and the intensification of the process of integration at least until 1965, involved a similar pattern of response from Moscow; political attacks accompanied by proposals for an all-European Security Conference.[8] A basic continuity in the Soviet attitude to Western European integration efforts existed during this period. However, the tactics adopted by the Soviet Union varied more than this brief summary might suggest. From a doctrinal point of view Western European integration was defined, not as a permanent system produced by 'objective' economic forces, but a temporary 'subjective' formation, a part of the infrastructure of the anti-Soviet capitalist camp, led by American monopoly capital.

Until 1957 Soviet leaders could congratulate themselves that their diplomatic and propaganda broadsides aimed at the process of West European integration, had, in their judgement, met with partial success. The survival and development of the Coal and Steel Community could be shrugged off as a very small, even insignificant affair. But the implementation of the Treaty of Rome, the acceleration of the process of integration, and evidence of economic growth brought home to them that an attitude of outright opposition might be counterproductive.

Immediately before the conclusion of the Rome Treaty in 1957 the Soviet statements insisted that the Community was and could be no more than a temporary phenomenon; they based this view on Lenin's thesis in his 'On the Slogan of a United States of Europe' that the formation of the United States of Europe was either impossible or reactionary, and that an entente of this character would not overcome the internal contradictions of monopoly capitalism.[9] The 17 theses on the Common Market, issued by the Moscow Institute of World Economy and International Affairs in 1957, before the ratification of the Treaty of Rome came into effect, defined the ideological basis of the Soviet and Communist attitude to the Community until 1962. It did not deny that such a bloc could expand its internal market but forecast that 'no doubt the tensions and contradictions between the members of the European Economic Community will accelerate the process of capitalist self destruction'.[10] Events in 1959–60 seemed momentarily to confirm this diagnosis. The American recession seemed to indicate the early dissolution of the EEC under the pressure of world economic crisis. There was no need to do much beyond waiting for the inevitable. The EEC was not an historical reality and need not be taken seriously. However, the actual progress of the first stage of customs union, the expansion of production and of internal trade in the EEC between 1958–1961 cast some doubt on these Soviet forecasts.

The Soviet debate on the nature and direction of European integration, 1961–69

The debate which opened in 1962 was occasioned partly by the reaction in Moscow to the Community's continued existence and signs of strength and to some extent also by the attitude of the Italian communists and Marxist economists from both Eastern and Western Europe. The conference of economic scientists from 23 communist countries met to discuss the problem. Their dilemma was how to admit the reality of the Western integration process, while maintaining that it did not invalidate the thesis of the objective contradictions of capitalism. The 32 theses, which were published before the conference together with a statement by Krushchev, restated the ideological position. They implicitly recognised the EEC as an economic and political reality. Krushchev, however, appeared to go somewhat further. He warned that 'while the possibilities of this international organisation should not be exaggerated, not to overestimate the capabilities of the enemy or opponent, does not mean that one should ignore them. It would be imprudent and short sighted were we to pay no heed to the planned activities of the advocates of European integration — we note the objective tendencies towards the internationalisation of production, which are occurring in the capitalist world, and which determine policy and economic measures'. [11]

The chief concern of the conference was to reconcile the reality of European integration with the doctrinal tenets of Marxism — Leninism. It required an emphasis on the thesis that the integration of capitalist states was a higher stage historically than contradictions between them. Krushchev's statement implied that the final stage of capitalism was not characterised by destructive national contradictions, but rather by integration in the face of the more fundamental contradiction — between capitalism and socialism. This has been interpreted as a denial of basic Leninist dogma, but this ignores the distinction between the strategic and tactical doctrines to meet changes in political conditions. Communist ideological positions have in the past fluctuated between emphasising contradictions within capitalism and the tendency of capitalist states to combine against the Soviet Union. The main impetus to the reformulation of the doctrinal position came from the realisation that the EEC was more than a transient phenomenon and that consequently a reappraisal of policy was required. It was necessary to contain the EEC, to prevent its expansion to include additional members, and embrace large numbers of developing countries in one bloc.

The sensitiveness of Soviet leaders to fluctuations in the process of European integration, and changes in the wider international system were illustrated by their response to the protracted crisis of the Community, which commenced with de Gaulle's veto on British entry in 1963 and attained its climax in the conflict between France and the Five during the year 1965/66. It revived doubts about the reality and permanence of the Community. Soviet assessments of the EEC since 1963 seemed to revert to the thesis that the EEC as an association of capitalist states was particularly vulnerable to internal contradictions and might perhaps prove to be a transient phenomenon. The impossibility of capitalist integration had been demonstrated. The Common Market was not based on any inevitable process of the internationalisation of production — and thus was not an economic reality. In the aftermath of the 1965/66 Brussels crisis the prospects for political integration seemed to the Soviet, with some justification, to be remote; therefore the market could only be a political device, part of the Western superstructure and consequently an anti-Soviet instrument.[12]

It was not surprising that Soviet reaction to the renewed British effort to seek entry to the EEC was hostile. It directed its propaganda to those anti-market groups in the Labour Party, claiming that British membership was in the interests of monopoly capital, but that the EEC itself was a façade for the domination of US monopoly capitalists and in direct opposition to the true interests of Britain, which could only be served by all European economic cooperation. [13] A restatement of the ideological position *vis-à-vis* European integration to a communist world conference in June 1969 seemed to echo some of the propositions of the 17 theses of 1957. It was claimed that imperialist integration would revive antagonistic social conflicts on an ever increasing scale and intensity, and lead to additional contradictions. 'The European bourgeoisie had embarked on an attempt to create stable and permanent institutions among capitalist states despite imperialist contradictions. However these contradictions cannot be overcome while imperialism continues to exist'. [14] This indirect and oblique indication of a revised attitude, combined with reaffirmation of orthodox doctrine, continued to characterise the Soviet attitude towards the EEC. West European integration was explained as the 'objective' tendency towards the internationalisation of productive forces. Simultaneously, however, it was stressed that the capitalist crisis was deepening and was bound eventually to lead to the break-up of the system. Apparently the Soviet leadership was anxious to avoid taking up a position which would compromise the long term thesis that capitalism would collapse from its own internal contradictions, while at the same time retaining sufficient doctrinal flexibility to permit tactical adaptations of policy to meet a fluid situation. It was aimed at keeping open as many options as possible. Were the Community to show signs of serious internal strains, then the ephemeral character of capitalist integration could be emphasised; were Community solidarity and cohesion to increase, then the internationalisation of the forces of production as an 'objective' process would be given greater prominence. If it was based on the latter, then it was an economic reality, which need not halt at the Oder–Neisse line, but would spread to the rest of Europe. If however it did stop at that point, that proved that it was not an economic reality, but a 'subjective' device — namely Western political unification aimed at the Soviet Union and the socialist camp. However, both are potential threats to the Soviet Union.

The more relaxed Soviet attitude towards the EEC, 1970 onwards

Two events in the early 1970s resulted in a more relaxed attitude on the part of the Soviet Union towards the European Community. First, the emergence of the Brandt government, committed to establishing a new relationship with the Soviet Union and her allies; second, the enlargement of the community and particularly the entry of Britain.

Until 1969 Soviet propaganda had attacked West German revanchism and expansionism, though with varying degrees of virulence, and had for good measure charged the Community with being either a willing vehicle or a helpless instrument thereof. However, the Bonn—Moscow and Bonn—Warsaw treaties of 1970 made the continuation of that propaganda line no longer credible or necessary. Later in 1972 the conclusion of the *Grundvertrag* between the two Germanies set the seal of recognition on the German and the Eastern European *status quo*, thereby achieving an objective pursued by the Soviet Union since 1958. It also registered in formal terms the Soviet—West German *rapprochement,* and represented a further stage in the development of the East—West détente. Furthermore, it created the conditions for a more positive attitude to the Community on the part of the Soviet government and party.

Though the Soviet Union had opposed British attempts to seek admission to the EEC in 1961 and again in 1967 and in 1970, once British membership was an accomplished fact the Soviet Union appeared to regard this as evidence that the Community was indeed an economic reality, and part of a permanent 'objective' process of integration. Moscow now defined peaceful coexistence more in terms of economic cooperation between the different systems. It was claimed that despite the existence of two opposed economic systems, the world economy continued to exist and function; the world economy was defined in terms of Marxist—Leninist doctrine as the totality of two separate and opposing economic systems which are nevertheless linked together in a particular way, each influencing and being influenced by the other. There existed between the socialist and capitalist world economics a division of labour. This concept of a division of labour implied that intersystem cooperation could not develop until and unless the 'objective' character of European integration was recognised. This subtle revision, or perhaps more accurately rein- terpretation of communist doctrine created the basis for a shift of Soviet policy towards the EEC. It justified intersystem cooperation between the EEC and CMEA. At the same time, however, European integration continued to be described as temporary in the long term, and not invalidating in any way the thesis of the ultimate demise of capitalism. The Soviet leaders adopted a formula giving themselves the opportunity to move as far towards recognising the EEC as circumstances and Soviet political and strategic interests dictated.

Brezhnev's speech to the 15th Congress of Soviet Trade Unions on 20 March 1972 tentatively and cautiously spelt out the revised position.

> The Soviet Union by no means ignores the real situation which has emerged in Western Europe, including the existence of an economic grouping of capitalist countries as the Common Market. We are carefully observing the activity of the Common Market and its evolution. Our relations with the participants in the grouping will, needless to say, depend on the extent to which they recognise the realities obtaining in the socialist part of Europe, particularly the interests of the member countries of the Council for Mutual Economic Assistance. We are for equality in economic relations and against discrimination.[15]

Neil McInnes rightly points out that Brezhnev said substantially no more in 1972 than Krushchev had said ten years earlier.[16] However, while the latter's statement was followed in 1963 by a renewal of the hardline position, Brezhnev's speech to some extent registered the more relaxed attitude to the EEC which developed in 1970.

Later statements in Moscow seemed to indicate that the Soviet Union seemed now to accept the 'objective' economic reality of the EEC. In a speech on the 50th anniversary of the Soviet Union Brezhnev asked:

> Is it possible to find a basis for some form of business relations between these intergovernmental trade and economic organisations now existing in Europe — between the CMEA and the Common Market? The answer is probably yes, if the states that are members of the Common Market refrain from all attempts at discrimination against the other side and if they promote the development of national bilateral ties and all-European cooperation.[17]

The *Guardian* reported an invitation from Comecon's Secretary-General, Nicolai Fadayev, to the EEC for top level talks. The impression was that

47

he wished to have discussions with the President of the Commission, Mr Ortoli.[18] Clearly a major reason for this initiative is the fact that in January 1975 the Community's common commercial policy came into force and subsequent negotiations for trade agreements have to take place with the Community as such rather than with individual member states. Most trade agreements as distinct from cooperation agreements between Eastern European countries and community members expired at the end of 1974.

The concern of Soviet spokesmen to maintain the basic premise that capitalism could not ultimately avoid the consequences of its internal contradictions while defending the legitimacy of recognising the reality of intergration, is revealed in a recent article in *New Times*. In a perceptive and well informed analysis of the present state of the European Community, the writer describes capitalist integration as a multistorey structure: on the ground floor, a customs union; on the first floor, common manpower and capital markets; on the top floor, economic and monetary union.

> While the first floor has been firmly established, and some, though incomplete progress, has been made on the first floor, no success has been achieved in setting up the second floor. In the last few years EEC has at most been marking time, but in some respects, in monetary cooperation, it has nearly regressed. It would be an exaggeration to claim that EEC is disintegrating . . .

The writer also remarks, significantly, that

> . . . national economies have become too closely interlocked, and European business sufficiently integrated, to permit a return to the situation prior to the establishment of the Common Market. The process of integration, objectively necessitated by the development of the productive forces is bound to go on. It may be retarded, but it cannot stop just as the process of social production cannot stop.

But then, as if to reconcile this with the basic Marxist–Leninist position, he adds,

> But this is not to minimise the significance of the present crisis of the EEC — no matter how it tries to adapt to present conditions, capitalism cannot rid itself of the inherent difficulties and contradictions from which it suffers.[19]

This Soviet ambivalence between confidence in the long term evolution of the socio-economic system and a distinct lack of certainty concerning the way in which events will develop in the short term and the tactics to be adopted to meet them is characteristic of contemporary Soviet policy. But the apparent readiness to accept the Community as a part of the European political scene for the time being, as well as the cautious ideological preparation for a possible decision to recognise the Community, suggests that the Soviet leadership had been engaged in a continuing reappraisal of the role of the enlarged Community in the Western world and its significance for Soviet foreign policy.

Détente and the Soviet Union's attitude towards the EEC

The Soviet attitude to the Community has to be seen in the context of détente, or from the Soviet perspective, of 'peaceful coexistence', since détente is a term more generally used in the West. It requires some assessment of the aims of Soviet peaceful coexistence or the policy of a 'limited opening to the West' as it is sometimes described. Its first objective is to strengthen the special relationship with the USA, which remains an adversary partnership with competitive and cooperative elements. The Soviet Union wishes to reinforce the relationship with agreements on strategic weapons (SALT) and tacit procedures for crisis management of conflicts which might lead to nuclear conflict, which the Soviet Union as well as the USA wishes to avoid. Upon the special and exclusive bipolar relationship rests the Soviet superpower role. A multipolar or pentagonal world system has no attraction for the Soviet Union. It would mean a relative reduction in status and influence, and would place her in a minority in the councils of the world and might also complicate the process and prospects of conflict management.

Second, the Soviet leaders, subject to economic pressures from within, are anxious to obtain capital and technological facilities from the USA and Western Europe. However, they are not prepared to accept conditions which would be seen to be discriminatory or constitute intervention in the domestic affairs of the Soviet Union.

Third, they seek to obtain from the West recognition of the *status quo* in Eastern Europe established at the end of World War II, including the territorial gains made by the Soviet Union. One of the purposes of the CSCE, and undoubtedly one reason why the Soviet Union lays such stress on a full summit conference to sign any agreements which emerge from the negotiations, is to secure such recognition from the Western powers. It is a part of Moscow's determination to maintain the stability and security of Eastern Europe, and insulate it as far as possible from the disruptive and disintegrating influences which détente might produce.

Fourth, the Soviet Union wishes to create a favourable image and reputation as a peace loving and cooperative state. The creation of a psychology of détente would compound the problems facing Western governments in maintaining existing levels of defence during a period of rapid inflation, in face of the competing demands for social welfare expenditure.

Western Europe is, and is likely to remain, an area of major priority for the Soviet Union, because it constitutes the largest concentration of economic wealth, power and industrial efficiency after the United States, and includes the most powerful of the German states, whose capability and intentions will always be the concern of Soviet leaders, even if the German problem has been resolved in a manner which satisfies Soviet interests. The successive treaties between the Federal Republic on the one hand, and the Soviet Union, Poland, Czechoslovakia and finally the German Democratic Republic on the other, taken together with the Four Power Agreement on Berlin, constitute a sort of ersatz peace treaty. Moscow has achieved the aim she has sought since the end of World War II, the formal registration of the political and territorial situation created by her defeat of Germany in Central and Eastern Europe. That her ambitions extend further is not doubted by most students of Soviet policy. Differences exist concerning the nature of these ambitions, and the tactics likely to be employed to attain them.

The Soviet Union has always regarded itself, and has been so regarded by others at most times, as a great European power. It considers itself entitled to exercise at least substantial influence throughout the continent, the more so today, since it has achieved the exalted rank of a world power. As such it would claim the right to a say in the affairs of Western Europe. Even though the overt use of military force by the Soviet Union to impose direct control over Western Europe is unlikely, it cannot be entirely excluded in certain exceptional circumstances, and Soviet leaders are not likely to refrain from the use of superior military capability as an instrument of political pressure and persuasion. A view frequently expressed is that détente or 'peaceful existence' is a means by which the Soviets hope gradually to shift the European balance of power decisively in their favour, and that they will exploit every opportunity to do so, as long as no disproportionate risk, such as general war, is involved.

The emergence of a powerful political and military union in Western Europe would be a serious obstacle to the attainment of that goal. If the Western European integration process were to proceed to the stage of an autonomous European power with a unified decision making authority, it would pose very grave questions for the future leaders of the Soviet Union. There is a very strong case for saying that the dissolution or at least the undermining of the cohesion of the Community is a maximum objective of the Soviet Union, in terms of its political and strategic interests. However, maximum objectives are often only attainable, if at all, in the long term. The enlargement of the Community may have convinced the Soviet leaders for the time being that the containment of the Community is a more realistic objective. Indeed, it may even be the case that the disintegration of the Community in the short term would not be in the Soviet interest, particularly if it could only be achieved at unacceptable cost to other equally important Soviet interests, such as the containment of West Germany or profitable commercial deals. However, calculations of balance of risks and gains could easily be reappraised should a new situation develop.

Soviet leaders have probably concluded for the time being that the most effective and least costly way of preventing the possible emergence of a politically and militarily integrated Western Europe is to adopt a more positive posture towards the European Community in its present form. Recognition of and cooperation with an EEC which has reached the relatively modest level of a customs union, plus a very limited degree of economic integration, would not impose excessive disadvantages on the Soviet Union. Such a low profile attitude might, from their point of view, inhibit further integration far more effectively than a hostile attitude. This view might possibly be confirmed by their observation of Community experience since 1972: the failure to move substantially in the direction of economic and monetary union and the differences on many issues between the three power centres of the enlarged Community — Bonn, Paris and London. A more aggressive posture might stimulate the members of the EEC to greater integrative efforts. Nor would a relaxed attitude on its part prevent the Soviet Union from exploiting differences between the member states.[20]

How could the Soviet Union achieve a degree of political influence over Western Europe while diminishing any risk of reciprocal Western European influence over Eastern Europe? The continued maintenance of an asymmetry between the political movement and forces in the eastern and western halves of the continent is essential for the success of Soviet penetration of Western Europe. Two methods are possible: one perfectly legitimate, if the Western European states were willing to accept it, the other clandestine or at least illegitimate from the point of view of Western European countries. The first method would be the creation of a formal basis or machinery which would give the Soviet Union a legitimate right to be consulted in the affairs of Western Europe. The second would be a form of indirect subversion or disruption of the domestic systems of Western European states, through supporting the revolutionary activities and propaganda of the Western European communist parties. These methods are not mutually exclusive.

One of the aims of the Soviet Union in the CSCE negotiations was to secure for itself a legitimate (in the political sense) and, if possible, a formal right, to be consulted in Western Europe's affairs. In the preparatory conference stage and later there were tentative proposals for the creation of a more or less permanent European security organ, council or committee to implement any agreement arrived at. The initial implications and intentions of these proposals were that the organisation would gradually replace the existing alliances; but they later took on a more modest character. However, there have been signs that the Soviet Union has lately shown less enthusiasm, and does not appear to be pressing so strongly for the creation of such a permanent body. Some observers believe that Soviet ardour for this kind of agency has been cooled by the attempts of the Nine to obtain more concessions from the Soviet Union in the third basket of CSCE — cultural and individual freedom of movement.

Another possible legitimate procedure which might enable the Soviet Union to retain its control over the contacts of Eastern European states with Western Europe, as well as providing it with greater say in Western Europe, is to achieve mutual relations between the Community and CMEA, the intersystem cooperation which has become a frequent theme of Soviet writing in the last few years.

One of the major considerations affecting the Soviet attitude has been the maintenance of Soviet control in Eastern Europe, preventing the countries of Eastern Europe from being seduced by the attractions of trade and credits from the Community, which might encourage aspirations to a larger degree of independence. In recent months the East Europeans have been despatching technical delegations to Brussels or receiving Community officials at 'academic' seminars. The East Europeans, particularly the Hungarians, being more dependent on foreign trade than the Russians, have been more flexible in their attitude to the Community. They are clearly anxious to safeguard their markets in the West and their concern is probably one reason for the invitation by Comecon's Secretary General to the President of the EEC Commission to visit Moscow. This initiative has been interpreted as a move by the Soviet government to dissuade its East European allies from negotiating directly with the EEC. It is also the reason why the Soviets have moved further in the direction of recognising the EEC. As John Pinder observes in his contribution, [21] the Soviet leaders are edging towards a sort of mutual recognition and negotiation between the EEC and Comecon.

Such intersystem negotiations, particularly if they resulted in a trade agreement, would achieve three desirable goals from the Soviet point of view. First, the recognition by the Nine of Comecon, which would be implied, would complete the process of legitimising the European *status quo,* the first stage of which was concluded in the successive treaties between the Federal Republic, the Soviet Union and the other Eastern European states. Second, it would strengthen Moscow's control over the economic and trade policies of the individual member states of Comecon; third, if, as might well be the case, some organisations were set up to implement the agreement, it might possibly provide the Soviet Union with the opportunity to influence the economic and trade policies of Western Europe.

However, it appears that the Soviet government is under a misapprehension about the Community's willingness to negotiate on a bloc to bloc basis with the CMEA. There is no sign that the Community has changed its policy that it is only prepared to conclude trade agreements with individual Eastern European countries. Certainly the view of the Commission as expressed in two documents to the Council of Ministers is that Comecon is not an international organisation in the accepted sense, and possesses very little international legal personality. It considered that the Community could only envisage conducting with Comecon an exchange of information on matters of common interest. [22] If the Community Council of Ministers were to continue to adopt this position, the Soviet leaders would be confronted with a rather difficult choice between a limited opening to the West to secure for itself and the Eastern European countries access to credits and technological know-how, and the need to preserve its position of hegemony in Eastern Europe by ensuring the cohesion of the Warsaw Pact and the continued authority of the party élite through the reinforcement of ideological vigilance. Past experience would indicate that priority in the last resort would be given to the second objective. [23]

It is not possible to establish whether the Soviet Union sees any chance of modifying the power structure of the Community from within as a result of major changes in the internal policies of individual member states. It is difficult to speculate what would be the Soviet attitude were an Italian government which included the Italian Communist party to come to power. [24] There is no evidence that the Soviet leaders have yet considered adopting a strategy of infiltrating the Community from within through the Western European Community parties. On the other hand it would be premature to conclude that they would not support such a strategy if circumstances were favourable. [25] But it would depend on whether the Soviet Union had more to gain in financial and technological assistance from an economically dynamic community than in terms of political advantage from an unstable one.

Dilemmas facing the Soviet leaders in their attitude towards the EEC

The Soviet leaders face a number of dilemmas in their attitude to the EEC. First, they are clearly impressed by the development and enlargement of the Community into an economic and trading regional bloc with a population, economic wealth and productive capacity larger than their own, and by the penetration of EEC economic power and influence into Africa and the Mediterranean through the Association agreements. They seem to fluctuate between regarding the Community merely as a creature of the United States and American capital, and a grouping capable of independence from the USA. Soviet propaganda during the years 1969 to 1972 highlighted American support for British entry to the EEC as a part of the American attempt to strengthen her control of Western Europe. However, after British admission and particularly since 1973, they have noted with considerable satisfaction the evidence of differences between the members of the Community and the USA government on many issues, particularly in respect of the Middle East War and the energy crisis. [26] Exploitation by Moscow of the divergence of interests between the USA and the Community, and open encouragement of the supporters of a 'Europe for the Europeans' as against the Atlanticists among the countries of the EEC might be attractive as a tactical manoeuvre, but on the other hand it could risk provoking American distrust of the Soviet Union and disturb the dialogue between the two powers. However, there are some advantages for the Soviet Union in an economically powerful Western Europe, which could compete with and challenge the other two capitalist powers, the USA and Japan. It could be fitted into the communist strategy of exploiting the contradictions of world capitalism.

In so far as and as long as the Soviet leaders need financial credits and high-technology products from the West to increase the rate of development of their resources, the growth and efficiency of the economies of the Nine and the stability of the Community itself may continue to be sufficiently important to them to outweigh the political and propaganda advantages they might derive from any substantial deterioration in the economic condition in Western Europe. But the latter might give the Soviets increased leverage in relations with the Community. Although a policy of cooperation with the Community might encourage political and military integration, the Soviet leaders may calculate that the political, social and psychological climate at present prevailing among large segments of public opinion in Western Europe makes the prospect that the Community may develop as one of the independent centres of power in a pentagonal system highly unlikely. They have, moreover, made a distinction between an 'objective' process of economic integration and the transformation of the community into a political–military bloc, thus keeping open the option of opposing such a development, should it occur. Bearing in mind the conventional military capability which they are able to deploy within the framework of nuclear parity, it is probable that they believe that they could accept an economically wealthy but militarily relatively weak Western Europe with equanimity, the more so, if differences between the Community and the USA were to grow to such an extent as to impair mutual trust and confidence.

But that raises the question of the relative priority assigned by the Soviet Union to the special 'adversary partnership' relation with the USA and to its privileged superpower status and influence on the one hand, and the potential advantages of a Western Europe estranged from the USA on the other. If it is the case that Soviet leaders, despite their ideological commitment to a long term transformation of the international system, are cautious and conservative, they may be more inclined to give priority to their relationship with the USA, even if they do not at the same time neglect to play the political market for advantage. But it is to be expected that they will continue to pay every attention to developments in Western Europe and exploit every opportunity to expand their influence as and when possible.

A certain caveat has to be introduced here. Soviet leaders have been and continue to be preoccupied with changes in society; their ideology and body of doctrine are predicated on the dynamic character of history. This preoccupation makes them more aware than other national leaders of the need and obligation to assess constantly the impact of changes in the international environment on their objectives, strategy, and tactics. Recent reports and comments have suggested that the Soviet leadership has been engaged in a major reassessment of détente in the context of the economic crisis in the West. These reports were linked with speculation regarding the future of Brezhnev and the probability that a period of uncertainty about the eventual succession to the leadership was involved. There appears to be some disappointment with the fruits of détente in particular with the volume of credit and technological know-how from the USA and the conditions attached to trade exchange, which culminated in the Jackson demand for exit visas for the Jewish citizens wishing to emigrate to Israel, which prompted Soviet cancellation of the trade agreement. There appears to be a move to greater emphasis on self-sufficiency and on allocating greater priority to heavy industry over consumer goods industry. It is suggested that criticism is not aimed at the need for détente but at the concessions which have been made by the Soviet Union and may be required of it.[27]

The fundamental character of the contemporary constellation of power, and the apparent anxiety of Soviet leaders with respect to the challenge of Chinese hostility will continue to impel them to maintain the basic elements of their policy towards the West. The visit of Franz Josef Strauss to Peking and his cordial reception by Mao Tse Tung caused apprehension in Moscow about the possibility of future trends in EEC–Chinese cooperation. Although there are elements in the Soviet hierarchy, particularly in the security apparatus, the military establishment and the party organisation who may favour and press for a more radical change in Soviet policy towards the West, the balance would seem likely to shift rather towards a toughening up of the present line. However, several factors may cause the Soviet leaders to pause before deciding what course their policy should take towards the European Community and its members; the uncertainty about Britain's continuing membership of the EEC, the doubt about the outcome of the West German elections in 1976 and the identity and policy of the next Chancellor and government of the Federal Republic, and the economic and social trends in Western Europe.

Notes

[1] A. V. Sergiyev, *Science and Foreign Policy,* Znaniye Publishing House, Moscow, 1967, p. 32.

[2] G. Shakhnazarov, 'On the problem of correlation of forces in the world', *Kommunist,* February 1974.

[3] Ibid.

[4] Zbigniew Brzezinski, *Ideology and Power in Soviet Politics,* Thames and Hudson, London 1962, p. 102 and 103.

[5] Ibid., p. 107.

[6] See K. Booth, *The military instrument in Soviet foreign policy, 1917–72,* Royal United Services Institute for Defence Studies, London,

1973 and Herbert S. Dinerstein, *Fifty years of Soviet foreign policy*, Johns Hopkins Press, Washington Centre of Foreign Policy Research School of Advanced International Studies, The Johns Hopkins University, Studies in International Affairs, no. 6.

[7] See Malcolm Mackintosh, 'Moscow's view of the balance of Power', *The World Today,* March 1972.

[8] Proposals for a European security organisation were submitted by Soviet Foreign Minister Molotov to the four power conference of Foreign Ministers in Berlin in 1954.

[9] V. I. Lenin, *Collected Works,* vol. XIII, The Imperialist War, Martin Wishart, London 1930, p. 270.

[10] See Hans Bräker, 'Die Sowjetunion, China und die EWG', in *Politik und Zeitgeschichte, Beilage zur Wochenzeitung das Parlament,* B29/73, 21 July 1973, Bundeszentrale für politische Bildung, Bonn; and Charles Ransom, *The European Community and Eastern Europe,* chapter 3, Butterworths, London 1973 and David E. P. Forte, 'The response of Soviet foreign policy to the Common Market, 1957–63', *Soviet Studies,* vol. 19, 1967/8.

[11] N. S. Krushchev, 'Fundamental problems of the development of the Socialist World System', *Problems of Peace and Socialism,* vol. 9 no. 49, 1962, quoted in Hans Bräker, op.cit., p. 5.

[12] See Neil McInnes, 'The Communist Parties of Western Europe and the EEC', *World Today,* February 1974.

[13] V. Osipov. 'Problems and judgements across the Channel and then what?' *Izvestia,* 13 November 1969.

[14] Quoted in Theodor Schweissfurth, 'Sowjetunion, westeuropäische Integration und gesamteuropäische Zusammenarbeit; Ideologie und Machtpolitik in der sowjetischen Haltung zur EWG,' *Europa Archiv,* vol. 7, no. 8, 1972(1).

[15] L. L. Brezhnev, speech reported in *Pravda* and *Izvestia,* 21 March 1972.

[16] Neil McInnes, op.cit.

[17] Speech by L. L. Brezhnev on the 50th Anniversary of the USSR, reported in *Pravda* and *Izvestia,* 22 December 1972.

[18] The *Guardian*, 31 October 1974.

[19] Yuri Shishkov, 'The Malaise of the Common Market', *New Times,* Moscow, November 1974.

[20] A recent article in *Pravda* emphasises the divergences within the Community. 'The Community has been plagued by a number of problems that have substantially undermined its unity. In almost all fields — from the energy famine to agricultural policies — the countries of the EEC

despite the association's recommendations, have preferred to seek their own ways out of the impasse'. Vladimir Drobkov, 'In a disputations atmosphere', *Pravda* 27 October 1974.

21 See Chapter 5, pp. 71–91, 'How active will the Community be in East–West economic relations?'

22 *The Economist* 5 October 1974. On 1 February 1975 *The Economist* reported that Edmund Wellenstein, the Commissions's Director-General for external relations would be visiting Moscow in the following week to meet the Head of the Comecon foreign trade department, Moyseyenko, to prepare for the visit later in the year by the President of the Commission, M. Francois Xavier Ortoli.

23 See Karl Birnbaum, 'Die Genfer Phase der Konferenz über Sicherheit und Zusammenarbeit in Europa: ein Zwischenbilanz', *Europa Archiv,* vol. 29, no. 10, 25 May 1974.

24 For the attitude of Western European Communist Parties to the Community, see Neil McInnes, *World Today,* February 1974.

25 However, last year, Boris N. Ponomarev, CPSU, CC Secretary for relations with non-ruling Communist parties was reported as speaking of the need for Communists to be prepared to promote revolution in the West. Quoted in Walter C. Clemens, Jr., 'The impact of détente on Chinese and Soviet Communism', *Journal of International Affairs,* School of International Affairs, Columbia University, vol. 28, no. 2, 1974, p. 141.

26 See Yu. Ryzhov, 'In search of a Common Policy', *Izvestia,* 8 February 1974; Yevgeny Rusakov, 'New Round', *Pravda,* 19 March 1974, noted the decision of the EEC countries to open direct talks with the Arab oil producing countries, and commented: 'Bickering over oil is only part of a persistent struggle between the USA and EEC... A new round in the transatlantic struggle has now begun... Washington's postponement of the conference to work out a declaration on relations between the USA and EEC is considered to be an expression of dissatisfaction with the Common Market resolution'. See also L. Volodin, 'Atlantic Strife', *Izvestia,* 7 March 1974.

27 See Wolfgang Leonhard, 'Entspannung in Moll. Westpolitik wird überprüft – Führungswechsel im Kreml vorbereitet', *Die Zeit,* 24 January 1975; and Astrid von Borcke, 'Der Kreml und die Politik der Entspannung Machtkonstellationen und Richtungskämpfe' in *Politik und Zeitgeschichte; Beilage zur Wochenzeitung das Parlament,* B45/74, 9 November 1974.

4 A Common Foreign Policy or Coordination of Foreign Policies: Problems, Implications and Prospects

Frans A. M. Alting von GEUSAU

In the postwar period West European unification has been conceived interchangeably as an effort to overcome past divisions (Franco–German reconciliation), to regain world influence, to join the USA in meeting a Soviet threat and to pursue the inner dynamics of economic integration. In recent years, we appear to be in search of a European 'identity' as a response to the end of the cold war and the emergence of an American–Western European adversary relationship.

The summit Conferences of the Community in 1969 (The Hague) and of the enlarged Community in 1972 (Paris) may well have marked an important turning point in the postwar history of European unification. By emphasising the search for a European identity, the European leaders have apparently given priority to their efforts to regain world influence over any other considerations. The pursuit of European unification by summit diplomacy in fact entails the abandonment of earlier efforts to federalise Europe through a process of political integration, in favour of efforts to concert national policies through processes of intergovernmental coordination and consultation.[1]

During the recent world crisis, following the fourth Arab–Israeli war of October 1973, the 'new Europe' so conceived has been severely challenged in two respects. The European Community members have not exerted any 'world influence' in the Middle East conflict. Confronted with the energy crisis, the 1973 Summit Conference in Copenhagen has been unable to concert member states' policies.

How could this new Europe emerge from the ashes of functional federalism and the federal goals of the 1950s? And what does it imply for the present and future conduct of its relations with Eastern Europe?

To answer those questions and to speculate about the prospects for common or coordinated European foreign policies toward Eastern

Europe, we should briefly review and appraise the interplay between conceptions and policies in the history of European unification; we should analyse the rules by which these relations are being conducted; and we should distinguish the relevant areas in which an Ostpolitik is to be considered.

Conceptions and policies: an historical perspective[2]

Policies and political conceptions are not the effects of external circumstances, but responses to external challenges.

It is generally held that European unification took off as a response to the historical challenge of European wars and conflicts of the past and the actual threat of Soviet domination. Both challenges were assumed to contribute towards a process of federation building in Western Europe.

In an historical perspective, this set of assumptions could be seriously questioned. In 1950, Schumann was no doubt motivated by a policy of Franco–German reconciliation in launching ECSC. Conflict between parochial European states, however, had ceased to be the dominant issue in postwar relations. In fact, it was no longer relevant in the context of the developing bipolar confrontation between the USA and the USSR.

In a period of less than three years (1945–1948) the European continent became divided into a Soviet and an American sphere of influence – satellites in the East and protected partners in the West – and from 1947 onwards 'the cold war became primarily an American–Soviet affair'.[3]

The fundamental challenge to Europe after the 1945 breakdown was not a Soviet threat but the division of Europe. European federalists in the early postwar years indeed advocated a response to this challenge. At the time European unification became a policy, the Western European policy makers chose to accept American leadership – i.e. European division – as a condition for launching such unification. To the extent they perceived a Soviet threat, they left it almost entirely to the USA to deal with it. As late as 1973 and in spite of détente and Ostpolitik, European policy makers ultimately withdrew from the challenge of European division for the benefit of continuing American protection.

It is true that President de Gaulle of France had taken détente in the 1960s as a chance to overcome European division. His historical understanding, however, was clouded by a tragically obsolete view of French *grandeur*. This view disrupted the European Communities and contributed to their degradation into a mechanism for bureaucratic bargaining and technocratic assistance. He left his successors in the confusing and contradictory position in which they are continuing to assert a European identity against the USA while at the same time seeking and requiring continued American protection. The conception originally held of a Europe unifying itself with a view to overcoming European division was thus abandoned at the very moment when Western European unification became practical policy.

As a consequence, the fundamental impediment to developing a common European policy towards Eastern Europe lies in the fact that Western European policy makers had abandoned the search for such a policy as early as the late 1940s.

The members of the European communities do not share (as does the USA) distinct common political objectives on which they can build a policy towards Eastern Europe. This absence of common objectives has also become manifest in the Conference on Security and Cooperation in Europe (CSCE). In spite of the adversary relationship between the Community and the US, the former possesses no strength of its own without cooperation with the latter.

The decision of Western European policy makers in the late 1940s to withdraw from the challenge of European division and to accept instead American protection and leadership also entailed far-reaching consequences for the ensuing process of·European unification. The originally federalist objective of building the institutions necessary for Europe as an active entity in international affairs was replaced by the conception of gradually moving states to accept federation through a process of economic integration. This method reflected the American approach to European unification (the Marshall Plan and the Organisation for European Economic Co-operation); it also fitted the wishes of many European leaders to see a full transfer of sovereignty postponed *sine die*. As long as Western Europe enjoyed and accepted full American protection, the absence of agreement on ends did not affect too much the continuation of the integration process and agreement on means to further it. Even the severe crisis following French rejection of a European Defence Community in 1954 could be overcome quickly with the *relance européenne* in 1955 and the admission of Germany to NATO by way of a revised Brussels Treaty (Western European Union).

It was both the brilliance and the tragedy of the founding fathers of EEC and Euratom that they achieved a new take-off so shortly after the 1954 crisis and that they launched a forceful process towards economic change without agreeing on the political ends to be served by the process. When de Gaulle in the early 1960s raised the problem of the ends to be served by the process, the conception of leaving the crucial political decisions to the outcome of economic processes manifested its inherent weakness especially as regards the conduct of external relations. The Community tumbled from one crisis into another. It emerged from them not as a new actor in international relations, but as a sub-system in permanent crisis about its external relations and its internal development.

The consequences of concentrating on economic means and integration processes, while neglecting political objectives, have been particularly harmful to the conduct of relations with Eastern Europe. When Western unity toward Eastern Europe began to erode under the combined impact of rising self-consciousness in the communities, bipolar détente, and American involvement in South East Asia, no political European organisation existed to counterbalance the resurgent nationalism in the Community member states. The division of Europe into an American and a Soviet sphere of influence, and American leadership in the West, had disguised the fact that the postwar spirit of reconciliation in Europe had died.

The Community crises of the 1960s produced a revival of old rivalries between the Western European states. As the former European Great Powers — France, Germany and Britain — had exchanged their prewar dominating world position for a postwar semi-dependence on the USA, their rivalry took the form of a competition for more influence and less dependence. Where European integration had been founded on common interests, their rivalry took the form of clashes over the future of the community (including British membership) and competition in economic relations with third countries. Eastern Europe after détente became the most interesting object of competition between Western European states. The common commercial policy of the European Community as prescribed by the EEC Treaty, and advocated by the Commission towards Eastern Europe especially, became the most conspicuous victim.[4]

As a consequence, two further basic impediments to developing a common policy towards Eastern Europe have emerged:

1   Economic interests turned out to be divisive rather than unifying in external relations. In the absence of agreed policy objectives, member states have bypassed the communities as the framework for elaborating commercial policies to revert to bilateral relations and intergovernmental or non-committal consultation.

2   Whenever the communities become involved in external relations, they represent the necessarily inward-looking and protectionist aspect of a system in permanent crisis, trying not to upset what has been agreed upon internally and with so much difficulty.

The unwillingness of member states to forego their parochial rivalries is thus reinforced by the reluctance of third, especially East European countries, to deal with the communities as such. In the continuing, though more limited, adversary relationship between East and West, the Soviet Union can only gain from rivalry within the Community.

In view of the early passing away of the postwar spirit of reconciliation and the disappearing attractiveness of joining the USA against a Soviet threat, the communities' external policies have come to be based on the desire to regain world influence and to pursue the inner dynamics of economic integration. The former desire, as we have seen, is inherently divisive; the latter has failed to spill over to the area of policies about external relations.

Policies and rules: common and coordinated external relations

Our previous discussion suggests that few conditions are met for the emergence of a common European Ostpolitik.

Faced with the East — in terms of a Soviet threat during the 1950s, and the new challenge of détente during the 1960s — the Community member governments have never appeared to act on the basis of perceived distinct and common interests. During the 1950s, their interests were not markedly distinct from those of the USA. Concerted policies towards the East were formulated in the framework of NATO. During the 1960s, the tendency to pursue divergent policies towards the East has been more markedly clear within the European communities than it had been in the broader Atlantic framework. During those two decades the efforts of the Six to concert overall foreign policy or to achieve political cooperation showed a record of tragic failure.[5]

The efforts underlined at least two basic facts. First, coordinated foreign policies are unlikely to emerge automatically or necessarily from a process of economic integration. Second, *none* of the Community member governments were willing to adopt 'the Community method' for dealing with issues of foreign policy. These two basic facts have remained unchanged in the enlarged European Community of the 1970s.

The formula adopted by the Nine for political cooperation and eventual European union is no more than a patched up system of political consultation whose basic rules are derived from the experiences of other interntional, intergovernmental organisations. As experiences of the Nine show, political consultation assures an exchange of views and regular communication. It does not preclude separate or unilateral action. It has been and still is a well known instrument in a variety of international organisations. It was so in the European concert of the nineteenth century. Political consultation has been provided for in most alliances, developing most markedly in NATO, and it is part of the deliberative processes in the United Nations. In all these examples, the record holds few promises for the European Community in an eventual effort to elaborate a common Ostpolitik.

Political consultation in the concert of Europe orginated from the desire of the Great Powers to settle political problems among themselves, with the exclusion of middle and small powers. This type of consultation has been revived in bilateral relations between great powers since the early 1970s. Its success depends on the unpredictability of a balance between the Great Powers and serves primarily the interests of major powers in maintaining a predominant position. The institutionalisation and the growing participation of lesser powers in consultation — the case of the United Nations — has negatively affected its outcome. In the postwar multilateral alliances, efforts have been made to convert consultation as a means of deciding on mutual assistance in case of war into a regular instrument for dealing with the international situation of foreign policy in general.

In NATO (as in the European Community) it has been assumed that better procedures and more regularity would improve the effectiveness of consultation. It was also assumed that the unwillingness of states to give up their freedom to act unilaterally could be talked away in regular meetings and special committees.

The assumptions, so far, have not been supported by the facts. Consultation has achieved modest results in preparing conferences (disarmament conferences, the European Security Conference for NATO). It has invariably failed when vital interests are at stake or crises are to be dealt with. Inside NATO and in relations between the major powers in general, the most apparent trend in consultation at present is a return to bilateral diplomacy.

Since 1969, the European communities have attempted to refine and develop their rules for political consultation. First, the rigid distinction between the conduct of the communities' external relations and the coordination of member states' foreign policies — a product of the crisis of the 1960s — has become blurred. Second, the procedures for regular meetings have been refined to involve all relevant policy making levels in a continuous dialogue. The consultative mechanism now includes the governmental leaders in regular summit meetings, the ministers for foreign affairs in quarterly meetings (since the Paris Summit in 1972), monthly meetings of the Directors-General for political affairs, permanent consultation between ambassadors and staff accredited to third countries and international organisations, and coordination of policies in international conferences.

At their Copenhagen Summit the leaders agreed to meet more frequently and in the future to meet immediately, whenever required by the international situation (i.e. in crises). If one adds to this already impressive list the regular and special sessions of the Council of Ministers of the Communities dealing *inter alia* with external economic relations and frequent bilateral contacts between governments, the consultative can be termed the most advanced mechanism in interstate relations.

The basic rule of political consultation — i.e. an exchange of views without any obligation to give up separate or unilateral action — has been maintained, however. This was made clear again by President Pompidou in his comments following the 1973 Copenhagen Summit meeting. He noted with satisfaction that Europe had proved willing to proceed towards 'a Europe in which the states would not see their personality and their essential interests sacrificed'.[6]

As I have already noted, the elaboration of the new mechanisms for political consultation since 1969 is related to the search for a European identity. It would be erroneous to think, however, that this concept could become the foundation for formulating common political objectives or common policies. As the declarations of the latest 1973 Summit Conference have shown, no alteration to the basic rules for political consultation are envisaged. As far as the search for a European identity reflects the substance of external relations, it is no more than an exercise in frustration over European impotence and irritation with American predominance.

Talk about a European identity, like talk about the 'personality of its member states' may help political leaders to feel great at home. In the realities of power politics in the international system of the 1970s, they are no more than empty — if not dangerously self-deceiving — slogans. A European identity can only result from a completely unified European foreign policy, based on common and distinct objectives and policies in strategy, defence, diplomacy, crisis management, economic and cultural/ scientific relations. Such an identity is far from being a reality, especially in relations between the Community and Eastern Europe. In the absence of adequate rules and mechanisms for conducting a common Ostpolitik, we should now turn to the areas in which such an Ostpolitik is under review or should be considered.

Policies, rules and areas: a record of conflicts and neglect

A perusal of East—West relations in the 1970s indicates a broad range of relevant areas and issues for developing a common Ostpolitik. If one takes recent developments and the agenda of the CSCE as an indication, the following tentative list of areas and issues could be listed for the purpose of our analysis.[7]

1 *East—West reconciliation* In this area a European Ostpolitik is faced with a variety of ever-changing issues like relations between the two Germanys, developing ground rules for peaceful coexistence and the development of a more adequate network of bilateral, multilateral and institutionalised relations in the European region as a whole.

2 *European security* This area would include the broad issues of national and European defence policies and the possible evolution of a system of alliances towards a system of European collective security. It would furthermore include such issues as crisis management, the settlement of disputes and arms control and disarmament for all types of weapons (from nuclear to conventional).

3 *Economic cooperation* This area, as is made clear in John Pinder's contribution, includes a broad variety of issues. In this tentative list I would especially retain the issues of East—West reconciliation; trade (in agricultural, industrial products and raw materials, export credit insurance, liberalisation measures); industrial and technical co-operation; monetary relations; the developments of ground rules for economic relations between states with different economic systems; and the type of relations to be sought between states and/or sub-regional organisations, including the role of the Economic Commission for Europe (ECE).[8]

4 *The impact of science and technology* In this area, we could retain in particular such issues as the transfer of technology, the control of the environment, and communication and information systems.

5 *Human contacts and cultural/scientific exchanges* Whereas most of our governments have become major actors in international cultural relations, this area would include both questions of principle (attitudes towards state controlled exchanges, bilateralism versus multilateralisation, freedom of human contacts, suppression of freedom of expression) and practical issues (e.g. university exchange programmes, cultural centres, exhibitions, sports, tourism).

A comparison of these areas and issues with the actual progress made in elaborating a common or coordinated Ostpolitik leads to disturbing conclusions. The European Community and its members have not only failed so far to agree on policies and to devise adequate rules and mechanisms. They have simply neglected their responsibility to elaborate a common or coordinated Ostpolitik in most relevant areas. It is in a comparison of relevant areas and actual policies that the three fundamental impediments to a common policy are most striking. In abandoning their search for a policy as early as the late 1940s, the political leaders in the European communities have become inward looking. By converting their process of economic integration without agreed ends into a system in permanent crisis struggling to survive, their Ostpolitik was reduced to an instrument for keeping the system going. As a consequence, the common Ostpolitik was limited to the short list of trade issues, discussed by John Pinder, where coordination was necessary for internal Community reasons. Coordination, moreover, takes the form primarily of mutual consultation rather than common policy making. Even within the area of economic cooperation, relations with Eastern Europe are as a rule conducted bilaterally. The other four areas listed above have been neglected.

The search for a European identity since 1969 and the emerging new Europe of intergovernmental consultation on all levels have no doubt broadened consultation between member states on East—West relations. The most conspicuous example of this broadening consultation is given in Crispin Tickell's chapter on 'The Enlarged Community and the European Security Conference' (p. 119—21).

The modest amount of cooperation among the Nine in Helsinki and Geneva, however, might well give us a false perspective on the chances for a common or coordinated Ostpolitik.

1   What the Nine have achieved so far in the CSCE has taken the character more of a coordination of convenience than an act of policy. The Nine have been making painstaking efforts to agree on proper procedures for coordination among themselves. There is no evidence of any deliberate effort to work out a common strategy or common policies for the new era of East—West negotiations.

2   The success or failure of the Nine cannot be easily assessed. It is largely disguised by the success or failure of coordination in the larger NATO framework. In the particular setting of the CSCE — and given the absence of a distinct European policy — the Nine possess no strength of their own, as we have already seen without the USA and outside the NATO framework.

3   The very character of the CSCE itself could easily give us a false perspective on the political achievements of the Nine. The slow pace of

the Conference and the absence of meaningful results so far are ideally suited to a system in permanent crisis. It gives ample time to apply the cumbersome procedures for consultation, without ever putting the system to the test.

As a consequence, it would at least be premature to see the functioning of the Nine in the framework of CSCE as a significant step toward a common Ostpolitik.

Prospects for a common Ostpolitik

The outlook does not appear to be very promising. The fundamental condition for such a policy — common objectives and common policies — has never been met. The process of economic integration has not had the expected effect of forcing members into such a policy. Economic interests without shared political objectives have turned out to be divisive rather than unifying.

The rules and mechanisms devised for coordinating policies have so far proved inadequate. There is little reason to assume that the new mechanism of intergovernmental consultation holds out significantly better promises than the old 'Community method'. Its achievements in the CSCE offer a false perspective for its potential contribution towards a common policy. Political mechanisms and structures prove their worth when tested in a serious crisis. The failure of the Nine to deal adequately with the energy crisis in the wake of the 1973 Middle East War is a more significant, though ominous, indication of the adequacy or inadequacy of the mechanism. If the European policy makers indeed believed — as they declared in December 1973 — in the necessity of European union in order 'to assure the survival of their common civilisation', their response to the perceived threat does not hold any promises for the lesser need of a common Ostpolitik.

There is no reason, though, to be concerned about this. European policy makers have long ago reverted to the practice of issuing hollow declarations, for lack of substantial agreements. They are not likely to believe that our common civilisation is being threatened. They are more likely to believe that they can afford to muddle through, disunited among themselves, sometimes irritated by the Americans, but always in the surprise-free world of continuing US protection, Soviet reasonableness and unproductive East—West conferences. In such a world, they might indeed be able to muddle through à neuf and to be talked about as an entity sui *generis.* But no common or even coordinated Ostpolitik will emerge from it. It is all too likely indeed that in a surprise-free world, the sleeping dog — as John Pinder writes — will continue to lie. Nobody can tell, after the world energy crisis, how serious the next crisis must be to wake him up. But everybody can predict that by then it will be too late for a dog to run when it has already forgotten how to walk.

The prospects for a common Ostpolitik are a matter of imaginative political leadership and conscious political choice, whose continued absence there is good reason to fear. As leadership and imaginative policies are matters of human choice, the future remains intrinsically unpredicable, however. Experience can only teach us that imaginative policies require adequate institutions and mechanisms. In external relations a European Ostpolitik, nothing but full federal union — created by a political decision rather than emerging from a confusing process — has so far presented itself as viable.

Notes

[1] See Frans Alting von Geusau, 'The European Communities After the Hague Summit', Year Book of World Affairs, vol. 26, 1972, p. 35.

[2] This section summarises an analysis made elsewhere. See Frans Alting von Geusau, 'European Unification and the Changing International System: Retrospect and Prospect', in Frans Alting von Geusau (ed), *The External Relations of the European Communities: Perspectives, Policies and Responses,* Saxon House, D.C. Heath Ltd., 1974.

[3] Brzezinski, 'How the Cold War Was Played', *Foreign Affairs* October 1972, p. 184.

[4] See further Frans Alting von Geusau, *Beyond the European Community,* Sijthoff, Leyden, 1969. (Chapter VI).

[5] Ibid., chapters VI and VII.

[6] *Europe,* 21 December 1973, no. 1425. President Giscard d'Estaing's first press conference on 24 October 1974 made clear that the new President essentially follows the same line in foreign policy as his two predecessors.

[7] The list cannot be exhaustive of course; nor is it a fixed list. For a fuller treatment of issues see especially the contributions by John Pinder and J.C. Garnett, pp. 71—90 and 93—111.

[8] See e.g., Alting von Geusau and Morawiecki, *Sub-regional Organizations in Europe and the Changing European System* in the report published by the European Center of the Carnegie Endowment for International Peace under the same title in 1972.

5   How active will the Community be in East—West Economic Relations?

By John PINDER

In the first fifteen years after the Treaty of Rome came into force, the Community did little about its relations with the Soviet Union and Eastern Europe. It made a few special arrangements for some agricultural products and steel; took some steps to standardise export credit insurance; put the highest common factor in the member countries' liberalisation lists into a Community list and made any reimposition of a quota on a product in that list a matter for Community decision; applied the protocol on intra-German trade which allows tariff-free imports into the Federal Republic from the GDR; and fixed 1 January 1973 as the date after which no member government should conclude a new trade agreement.[1] Even if the list is not negligible, it remains unimpressive. With respect to East—West relations, the Community was inert.

There were two main reasons for this: the economic ideology of the Rome Treaty and of the Commission; and the political ideology of the member governments. The Treaty and the Commission both gave the strong impression that the main purpose of the Community was to create a perfect internal market; and if the interest in East—West trade is confined to the prevention of *détournements de commerce,* the policy is bound to be unimpressive. But economic thinking in the Community in general and the Commission in particular has now developed beyond this narrow view; and the political constraint has been relaxed as the Gaullist period has receded.

It is not that the member governments show enthusiasm for giving up their powers to the Community. But in 1974 they agreed to exchange information on their cooperation agreements with Eastern countries and the Community has, despite the British government's reserves about Community affairs pending the conclusion of the 'renegotiation', drawn up an outline trade agreement as a basis for negotiations with Eastern trading partners. The member governments have, moreover, managed to present a common front in the Conference on Security and Cooperation

71

in Europe, working through the intergovernmental procedures of the Davignon Committee, and thus considerably to enhance their influence on the Conference. Responding to the signs that the Community as such is becoming a factor in East—West relations, the Secretary General of Comecon has been authorised to make formal contacts first with the President of the Council and then with the President of the Commission of the Community.

There is, then, movement in the Community's relations with the Soviet Union and Eastern Europe; and it is natural to ask how far Community policy towards the East might go. First, however, we should consider how far we would want it to go. What useful purposes can be served by common Community policies?

The Community's economic relations with the Soviet Union and Eastern Europe are significant but not substantial. About 7 per cent of the Community imports or exports are with Comecon, and this represents more than ½ per cent but less than 1 per cent of the Community's income or gross domestic production. If all this trade were to cease, Community production, consumption, and trade with other areas would rapidly adjust with no noticeable effect on the general welfare. But particular branches of industry and commodity markets would have awkward adjustments to make; possibilities of future expansion in trade and industrial cooperation would be lost; and the volume of trade, while not enormous, is by no means negligible.

If the economic relations were only a matter of business, then, they would merit a place on the Community's agenda but not a high priority. But even if the economics of East—West relations are no more than significant, the politics are vital. Political and military relations with the Soviet Union are a matter of independence or constraint, and even of life or death. If economics can have influence on politics and security, the Community's relations with the East are of the utmost importance.

Political scientists can doubtless show with some professional rigour that politics and security are affected by economics. Here it is taken as a matter of simple common sense. It is also clear that the Community members are economically strong in relation to the superpowers but militarily weak, and that a major cause of this is that they are relatively united in economics whereas they are not united in defence, save through their links with the USA. It follows that the Community members would be wise to use their united economic strength to redress, as far as possible, the political advantage that the Soviet Union derives from its military preponderance.

Again, it is up to the political scientists to make a fine definition of the political objectives of Community members' policies towards the East. But for the purpose of this paper, these are crudely divided into two parts. First, there are the classic (though not *dépassé*) balance of power objectives: to move closer to political equality with the Soviet Union; and to help East Europeans maintain any degree of independence from the Soviet Union that they may be able to secure, without endangering peace. Second, there are modern objectives, with their roots in liberalism and democratic socialism, and their fruits in the international institutions and integration movements of the postwar period. Here the aim is to create the conditions for a more just and peaceful international order based on a political process and a rule of law within a system of institutions. It has been argued[2] that one such condition is a degree of pluralism within the participating countries. In relation to Eastern Europe and the Soviet Union, then, these modern objectives would imply more multilateral relationships, a greater recourse to international procedures and institutions, and the development of more open and pluralist tendencies in those societies.

The relationship between the classic and the modern objectives is complex; sometimes contradictory, sometimes independent, sometimes mutually reinforcing. But the distinction, if rough, seems a useful one to apply in considering the Community's economic policy and its political implications.

The classic ends and means of trade and cooperation agreements

The Russians have not welcomed the Community as a factor redressing the balance of power in Europe. They have opposed its creation and subsequent enlargement, and refused to recognise its legal right to have responsibility for the external trade of the member states. This line accords both with the pronounced classical vein in their foreign policy — Machiavelli could only have encouraged them to keep their smaller neighbours divided — and with the Marxist view that the Community can do no more than paper over the splits between its imperialist members who will eventually go to war with each other.

Neither the classical nor the Marxist analysis leads inevitably to that conclusion. For either could approve the creation of a second pillar of the Atlantic group which, so far from supporting the arch of the alliance, would crash against the American pillar and bring the arch tumbling down — if not a shooting war, at least a mutually destructive trade war between these two great imperialist blocs. Although they do not appear greatly

73

impressed by this ideological alternative, the Soviet leaders have nevertheless been able to put on their business hats and recognise that the Community has come to stay. Their pronouncements have, if only eliptically, indicated that recognition is possible.

The most favourable assumption is that as a result of the Conference on Security and Cooperation in Europe, setting a definitive seal on the recognition of European frontiers and states, the Soviet Union and its Comecon partners would recognise the Community and be ready to negotiate trade agreements and do other business with it. The guarded utterances of the Soviet leaders have, however, hinted that the price for recognition of the Community may be that it should do business with Comecon rather than with the Comecon member states. A common reaction to this idea in the Community, and among some East Europeans, is that it is a way to secure Soviet control over the external economic policies of the East European goverments, as part of a policy of locking the East European economies into an integrated economy with their great Comecon partner, in order to prevent them from straying into the same paths as the Czechs did in 1968. Comecon does not at present have a common external policy as the Community does; and this is not by chance, because whereas the major member states in the Community are of similar size so that none can dominate the whole, the Soviet Union is much more powerful than all the other members of Comecon combined, and would inevitably dominate a common external policy. The other members of Comecon tend to resist such an encroachment on their independence, so that Comecon remains without a common policy towards third countries.

Apart from the political objection that a Community trade agreement with Comecon could give the Russians a lever to strengthen their control over the East Europeans, there are two arguments to support a hardline response that the Community should either make trade agreements with individual countries or make none at all. One is that the East Europeans would not let themselves be pressed by the Soviet Union into making a common Comecon trade agreement; any such talk would be bluff and they would come round to individual dealings with the Community. The second is that trade agreements make little difference to trade. Western governments liberalise quotas because their industries can take it, not because of anything they get in exchange from negotiations; and the Eastern Governments offer in trade agreements nothing that they would not anyway give in the normal course of trade. There have been occasions when trade took place without trade agreements, and it appeared to flourish nevertheless. Even if the hard line resulted in no trade agreements, little or nothing would be lost.

But although the hard line would help to establish the Community as a powerful factor in political relations with the Soviet Union, it has its drawbacks. There are fears that détente could be checked or even reversed. A head-on confrontation with the Community might make it difficult for East Europeans to resist Russian arguments that a united Comecon front was the right response, even if the Community's intention was to avert such an outcome. Economically, there may be at least some mutual advantage to be found in the detail of the trade agreements; and trade agreements may influence the planners to favour trade with the other party to the agreement, even if there is no objective reason why this should be so. So the alternatives of hard and soft lines may present the Community with a dilemma. Is there a way through it?

A multilateral framework of principles with bilateral trade agreements?

The Russians have long proposed that East—West trade should take place within a framework of agreed general principles. They first proposed this in the Economic Commission for Europe in 1956. It was interpreted in the West as a device to forestall the integration proposed in Western Europe by setting up an all European system. The idea has been resuscitated from time to time and it could offer a way for the Community to deal with Comecon without precluding bilateral trade agreements on matters of substance between the Community and individual Eastern countries.

There will again be fears that such principles would be used to halt or reverse the integration in the Community, together with new fears that the Soviet Union could use them to strengthen its control over the East Europeans. But this of course depends on what the principles are. The Community and its members can reject any proposed principles that would hamper its own development; and though there are limits to the East Europeans' ability to resist Soviet pressure, the Community could also resist principles that seemed likely to increase substantially Soviet leverage in Eastern Europe.

If the list of principles was not such as to restrict the Community's development or the autonomy of East Europeans *vis-à-vis* the Soviet Union, it would seem immaterial whether they were negotiated by Comecon as a group or by the individual member states. For the Nine, they could be negotiated by the Community. Since America and Japan are now increasingly important in 'East—West' trade, it would seem appropriate that they too should participate in such negotiations; indeed, that all the members of Comecon and the OECD should take part. Having, in the course of the negotiations on these principles, secured due recognition of Comecon, the Soviet Union might more readily accept that East Europeans should have negotiations with the Community and make trade agreements with it about detailed questions of their bilateral trade with the Community.

It may be objected that these principles, even if they may be innocuous for the Community and the East Europeans, will still be of little use. There is some truth in this. Peter Wiles has shown[3] how Marxist analysis of international trade has been cramped by its narrow theoretical base; and it would be unrealistic to expect a very effective framework for East—West trade to stem from this source. Nor have liberal economists developed a powerful theory of economic relations between market and directive economies which could provide the kind of basis for trade between these economies that the liberal theories, embodied in the GATT, have provided for the trade among market economies.

Some practical benefits might nevertheless be derived from a statement of principles. Some of the provisions of bilateral trade agreements could perhaps be standardised in the form of multilaterally agreed procedures, without loss of significant freedom of choice for the individual countries; and this could remove some unnecessary complications from the tangle of bilateral agreements. Samuel Pisar has suggested that both Western and Eastern enterprises would benefit from 'a code of fair practices . . . operating to safeguard the general structure of world trade as it strains to accommodate the growing phenomenon of total state commerce' and has outlined the elements of such a code.[4] The Community could moreover strive to insert in the principles some openings for the development of multilateralism, convertibility and market mechanisms. This would be compatible with some of the aims expressed in Comecon's own Comprehensive Programme;[5] and it would point towards a development of trade in a way that 'need not be a matter of Sovietising East European economies but of Europeanising the Soviet economy'.[6] It will be a long time before there is significant progress in this direction in the Soviet Union; nor are further rapid changes in Eastern Europe likely, despite the success of the Hungarian guided market economy. But it is as well for policy makers in the Community to be aware that there are directions in which trade relations could develop that would be helpful for the autonomy of East European countries as well as for the more rational organisation of the trade itself; and the Community should be no less ready to promote such principles in international negotiations than the Russians are to put forward their own conceptions.

Even if, at the end of the day, there is not much to show for principles of negotiations in terms of either practical benefits in the short term or openings towards multilateral relations over the long term, an agreed list of principles would be worth negotiating if it did no more than pave the way for negotiations between the Community and the individual members of Comecon about detailed matters of mutual concern.

Community trade policy: quotas and safeguards

Whether the Comecon countries recognise the Community or not, and whether they negotiate trade agreements with it or not, the Community has decisions to take about its commercial policy towards them. One set of decisions concerns the element of subsidy in export credit terms, including the official insuring of export credits. Here the Community members have a common interest in not being manoeuvred by the Soviet Union and East Europeans into a competitive spiral of increasing subsidisation. There is already some Community coordination in this field and it was strengthened as a result of a recent Council decision.

But the main issue of commercial policy towards the East is tougher to resolve. Each member country has a number of quotas that restrict its imports of particular products from the Eastern trading partners. Except in Italy, the governments have eroded these restrictions until they protect only a hardcore of sectors, generally including textiles, but differing from country to country as regards the other sectors protected. These differences make it hard to agree upon common Community quotas.

From the viewpoint of external policy, this is a pity. For the relaxation of a Community quota could be quite a powerful instrument in dealings with Eastern Europe or the Soviet Union. It is therefore to be hoped that the member governments will be able to overcome the domestic difficulties which hinder agreements on a system of common quotas. But it is to be feared that they will not; and in this case events may point towards a solution which favours the modern, system-building, rather than the classical balance-of-power objectives of foreign policy.

One of the subjects in the current GATT negotiations is the definition of a regime of safeguards: the circumstances under which restrictions may be imposed on disruptive imports and the adjustment assistance which should facilitate their subsequent liberalisation. This system should be applied directly to the East European countries that are members of the GATT (Hungary, Poland and Romania as well as Yugoslavia). The Community could also apply the same system to its trade with other East European countries and the Soviet Union; or, if that system is not regarded as applicable to trade with the directive economies, the

Community could devise a special regime of safeguards for them (including those that are members of the GATT). This regime could be less liberal than the one to be applied to market economies in the GATT that undertake reciprocal obligations, but at the same time less arbitrary — and more *communautaire* — than the existing import quotas. This would provide an opportunity for discussions with the directive economies about their methods and practices of price formation, and hence for a rational consideration of the future development of relations between the new systems, as suggested later (p. 88).

While trade policy may point down an interesting avenue for the system builders, then, it seems to offer little towards the objectives of classical diplomacy. The tussle over recognition of the Community and its right to negotiate trade agreements is largely shadow boxing — though in this it may seem to the economist not that different from diplomatic activity relating to nuclear security, and in both cases the shadows are cast by heavy concentrations of power. If one is looking for Community negotiations that would come closer to the substance of East—West economic relations, however, it is worth examining the idea of a Community cooperation agreement.

Community cooperation agreements

Member governments in the Community, while not contesting the Community's right to negotiate on matters of commercial policy, have concluded long term 'cooperation agreements' with the Soviet Union and East European countries, which aim to encourage what has come to be called industrial cooperation between enterprises in the Western and Eastern countries that are parties to these bilateral agreements.

The term 'industrial cooperation' refers to transfers of finance, skills and technology: everything that lies between direct investment at one end of the spectrum and the exchange of goods at the other. Such transfers have grown enormously in importance in relations among the market economies, but until recently their relevance to relations with the Soviet Union and Eastern Europe was concealed by the fact that, within the West, they often take place under the umbrella of direct investment. Since in the Marxist economies the State is in principle the sole owner of the means of production, direct investment is not possible and the scope for these transfers was not understood. In the last few years, however, it has been realised that Western enterprises can be rewarded for their part in cooperation — for the transfers they make — in terms other than ownership of the means of production: that is, by payment of money or delivery of goods. Even if these devices are not a full substitute for simple ownership from the point of view of the Western enterprise, they will make it possible for East—West cooperation arrangements to expand in parallel with the growth of international investment in the West. So far from being a passing fashion, they represent a basic trend in the modern international economy.

National governments are therefore on to something important when they take an interest in this kind of cooperation. But just as trade agreements may not have much logical connexion with the actual trade, one has to ask what the governments contribute to cooperation between enterprises by concluding official cooperation agreements.

One answer is that such agreements may put the Eastern planners in a frame of mind in which they are readier to encourage specific agreements involving their country's enterprises, or that the work of the joint commissions which are established under such agreements can lead to the discovery of opportunities that would not otherwise be discovered. More concretely, the Western government may, as part of such an agreement, provide credit facilities for its firms that conclude cooperation agreements and make clear that such firms will have its diplomatic backing in dealing with the Eastern enterprises which, of course, automatically have the backing of the State because they are its property. But while the financial and diplomatic backing may well be essential to some deals which are perfectly good business even if the risk and effort for the State are added to the risk and effort for the firm, it is not evident that they need to be provided in the framework of a cooperation agreement, which could therefore be seen, like the trade agreements, as a function more of the Eastern planners psychology and of the shadow boxing of diplomacy than of objective economic necessity. As in the case of the trade agreements, however, the cooperation agreements are probably well worth having for these reasons, in addition to the more concrete policy measures on which they are based.

This being so, there are powerful reasons why the Community should have a cooperation policy and be ready to negotiate cooperation agreements. Most industrial cooperation projects are of a size which a single firm in a Community member country can handle without special government help. Some require the backing of the national government. But a few are so big that they are beyond the industrial and financial resources of a single member country. Some Soviet projects, in industries such as chemicals and petroleum extraction, require $5,000 million or more of finance from the West, as well as massive activity on the part of Western companies. For such projects, the resources of member countries

Siberian Pipeline

would have to be combined. Consortia of some of the largest West European firms would have to be formed, money raised from more than one capital market, and collective financial and diplomatic backing provided by governments.

The Community is the obvious vehicle for such ventures. The European Investment Bank could be the linchpin for the financing. The member governments' financial and diplomatic backing could be coordinated in the Community's institutions. The activities of the consortium could be coordinated by a European company which, when the Community's company statute has been agreed, the companies participating in the consortium could jointly establish and own. Alternatively, the Community could establish its own public enterprises to negotiate with the Eastern partners on behalf of the Western firms.

If the members of the Community do not combine their efforts, the big projects will go to the Americans or Japanese. There may consequently be pressure from industrial and financial interests for Community involvement. This coincides with the political interest of the Community countries in securing influence with the Soviet Union on the basis of their economic strength. These big projects may therefore offer an opportunity for the Community to do something important in relations with the Soviet Union and Eastern Europe in the fairly near future.

The Council's decision on industrial cooperation did not do much to pave the way for common action to enable the Community to take part in such projects, although the idea of the Community as such participating in cooperation arrangements did surface at one point in the Commission's communication to the Council on the subject.[7] The Council confined itself, however, to agreement on further measures to coordinate export credit terms and on the mutual exchange of information on member governments' own cooperation policies. It may be contended that consultation is a step to harmonisation, which is in turn a step towards common action taken with Community instruments; but it can also be argued that this is an unduly circuitous route to the establishment and use of common instruments, which is the most effective form of Community action.

The modern ends and means of convertibility and price reform

So far we have been seeking ways in which the Community could bring its economic strength to bear so as to influence the Soviet Union, with the classic aim of helping to redress the balance of power in Europe. Without prejudice to this legitimate and necessary purpose, one can ask whether the Soviet Union and Eastern Europe may come to accept more readily multilateral procedures and international institutions as the means of regulating their relations with other countries, and whether the Community can encourage them to do so.

The Marxist orthodoxy is that such cooperation or integration should take the form of intergovernmental collaboration between countries with directive economies, and that cooperation with market economies is a temporary expedient, pending the conversion of the market economies into directive economies. Only time can prove that this view is wrong; and meanwhile integration between the market economies is, in the Community, seen increasingly to require common or coordinated policies that are interventionist by the traditional standards of the market economy. But there is an impressive body of political science research which indicates that cooperation and integration are facilitated by the pluralist elements in the participating countries' systems. In economics, it is the market as distinct from the directive elements that are pluralist; and in the remainder of this chapter we accordingly consider whether the market elements in the East European and Soviet economies may increase; whether this can lead to more effective international procedures and institutions; and whether the Community can play a part in this process.

Can markets and Marxists coexist?

Oskar Lange was the first to argue that state ownership of the means of production was compatible with a market system.[8] The debate has continued during the last twenty years and in the last ten years all the Comecon countries have introduced economic reforms which employ some elements of the market mechanism.[9] Some of those who pressed the case for markets too hard have fallen into disgrace and exile.[10] The Czech reform was stopped in its tracks. On the other hand the Hungarians have, with their 'new economic mechanism', made more extensive use of market principles than any other Comecon country,[11] and the Yugoslavs, unconstrained by the presence of Russian troops in their country, have ventured still farther with the market economy — to the point where they have paid for their high rate of growth by sharing the Western worries of inflation and unemployment.

The economic reforms of the late 1960s were a consequence of the slowing down of economic growth in Comecon countries earlier in the decade. The same cause might well again produce a similar effect, and the growth of the Soviet economy has again decelerated in the early 1970s.

The search for Western technological and financial help is one result. Is a new decentralisation, perhaps even a Soviet 'new economic mechanism', another likely consequence?

This is not impossible, but it seems wise to assume that it will not come about unless there is a much deeper economic crisis, following reforms still based on the principles of the directive economy. For Soviet leaders will certainly fear that a relaxation of detailed economic controls would lead to a reduction of political control.

If the Hungarian guided market continues to be as successful as it has been so far, however, there is a fair prospect that the Poles, who see themselves at present steering a course between Hungary's market-oriented reform and the GDR's directive-oriented reform, will increasingly approach the Hungarian model. The Czechs, if they regain the capacity for creative developments, would probably do the same. The political leaders of the GDR, with their commitment to close alignment with the Soviet Union and sharp distinction from the Federal Republic, and with what seems to be the most efficient of the directive economies, seem unlikely to change unless the Soviet Union does; and Bulgaria and Romania are less developed and hence less prone to the problems that beset directive planners in advanced industrial economies. If, however, the Hungarians remain stable and prosperous and the Poles (and perhaps later the Czechs) were to approximate to their economic model, there would be a substantial area in Comecon with a type of economy that has been recognised by the GATT as substantially a market economy for the purposes of international trade.

In 1974 the Hungarians took measures that were interpreted by some as a reversal of their economic reform in response to Soviet pressure. A sounder interpretation is probably that internal forces in favour of maintaining the (reformed) *status quo,* with some minor reversals, prevailed over those who wanted more reform; and that the conservatives were backed by the Soviet Union. If this is correct, it does not seem likely that a further gradual development of market mechanisms in Poland would be prevented by Soviet pressure, provided that there are no dramatic lurches forward and that the economic evolution is not seen to be accompanied by disturbing political or ideological trends. Because of memories of such trends in Czechoslovakia, however, the Soviet constraint over the Czechs seems likely to remain tighter for some years ahead.

In considering the Community's response to any strengthening of market mechanisms in Eastern Europe, then, we are thinking about problems which already exist and may become more important. There is also the possibility, though hardly a probability, that the Russians would respond to a prolonged period of slow growth by important further steps towards economic decentralisation. The analysis, while it should stick to the nuts and bolts of economics, is lent a certain excitement by the hypothesis that more economic pluralism could offer a basis for a new and much more constructive economic relationship between Eastern and Western Europe.

Convertibility and multilateralism

East—West trade is based largely on the principle of bilateral balancing and on the inconvertibility of the Eastern currencies. It has often been pointed out that this severely restricts the operation of market principles and the actual level of trade. Many proposals have been made for moves towards convertibility and multilateralism, [12] but to discern the scope for action by the Community, one has to understand what are the obstacles to their achievement.

First, the Eastern planners may think in terms of bilateral balancing by force of habit, even if it is not really necessary. Trilateral or multilateral flows can in principle be organised by the planners, and have in practice operated in the cases of Finland with pairs of Comecon members, likewise some developing countries with Comecon pairs, and in the substantial case of the Russian use of sterling, earned from exports to Britain, to buy in other countries in the sterling area. The Comecon members have agreed, in principle, that they would like to move towards multilateralism and convertibility among themselves for the 1980s; [13] but it may be that habits of mind will have to change before they do so.

Second, there is the concrete difficulty that the demand for 'hard' (i.e. Western) currencies is much greater than the demand for 'soft' (i.e. Comecon) currencies, so that convertibility of Eastern into Western currencies would either have to be quickly suspended or would cause a massive depreciation of the Eastern currencies. For these reasons the East Europeans will not contemplate it until supply and demand seem to be in better balance. Reciprocating this Eastern refusal to allow their currencies to be converted, some Western countries have, although their currencies are in principle convertible, warned their East European partners that they had better not unbalance the trade by making excessive use of the convertibility.

Current rates of inflation in the West have the effect of a significant annual revaluation in relation to the Eastern currencies which might lead one to expect that the exchange rates would reach equilibrium after a few years. It is claimed, on the other side, that East European planners' and enterprises' demand for Western capital goods is inelastic and insatiable, so that exchange rate adjustment will not bring their demand for currency into balance with supply. If the trend to greater reliance on costs and prices as a regulator continues in Comecon, however, the force of this argument will diminish.

Third, most Comecon countries still have little confidence in the validity of their internal prices as an indicator of what should be bought and sold in external trade. As the Comprehensive Programme says, 'In the nearest future the CMEA member countries shall continue to apply the present principles underlying the determination of prices in their reciprocal trade, i.e. fix them on the basis of world prices after having neutralised the harmful influence exerted by the interplay of speculative forces on the capitalist market.'[14] They likewise usually sell their exports to market economies at the price levels existing in those markets. The difference between internal and external prices is adjusted by tax or subsidy, as is done by the Community for agricultural products under the common agricultural policy (CAP). Although this does not in principle prevent multilateral trade and convertibility, any more than the CAP does, it blunts enthusiasm for the use of these instruments of an international market economy, because it is hard to judge whether trade reflects a comparative advantage or not.

Fourth, it is often said that convertibility of currencies cannot precede convertibility of goods: even if you have enough of a Comecon currency, you cannot buy the goods you want from that country unless the planners agree; and if they have not put your purchase in their plan, they may not agree. This does not render the currency valueless, because you may be able to get what you want after a wait; some Comecon countries allow producers of some goods to manufacture what is ordered by the market (which may include foreign buyers) rather than solely according to instructions from the central plan. Thus you may be an importer with a fairly regular need for the currency or you may be able to sell it to somebody else who does have a need. But to the extent that goods are not unconditionally available, the 'moneyness' and hence the value of the currency is reduced.

For such reasons, the Comecon countries are going slow in their moves towards convertibility and multilateralism among themselves. Although the transferable rouble is used, this is more as a bookkeeping than as a financial unit. But it is intended to make progress during the 1970s, and 'the decision on the introduction of a single rate of exchange for the national currencies and on the date of its introduction shall be adopted in the course of 1980'.[15] The Comecon countries were already, in 1971–72, to 'study and prepare for implementation measures to make the collective currency (transferable rouble) convertible into the national currencies of the CMEA member countries and to make the national currencies mutually convertible'. [16] Further, in establishing economically well-founded rates of exchange or coefficients for the national currencies, the countries shall resolve, in accordance with their possibilities and conditions, questions relating to the correlation between domestic wholesale prices and foreign trade prices'. [17] Thus there is a serious intention to overcome the obstacles to convertibility and multilateralism in Comecon trade; and if this is done, it will become much easier to move in the same direction in East—West trade and payments.

The Comecon countries have indicated that they would like to be able to make some moves of this sort: 'As the collective currency (transferable rouble) begins to play a greater role it may ultimately, along with other currencies used for international settlements, be utilised for settlements with third countries and thus assume a place commensurate with the role and importance of the CMEA member countries in the world economy'. [18] When they are nearly ready for a measure of convertibility, the Community could help to finance it, as the United States helped to finance the European Payments Union in the postwar period.

Meanwhile, the Community could encourage a trend towards multilateralism in certain specific ways. It would investigate, in consultation with the Comecon countries, the scope for trilateral trade analogous to those flows mentioned above. The Community could, indeed, unilaterally offer multilateralism as far as its own members are concerned. It could, that is to say, invite the Comecon trading partners to use currency earned from exports to a Community member to buy goods anywhere in the Community. This would remove a distortion from the Community's internal market, and set a precedent for the growth of multilateralism and convertibility where they are practicable.

Useful though this would be, one could not expect the Comecon countries to reciprocate fully until they had resolved those 'questions relating to the correlation between domestic wholesale prices and foreign trade prices', and had in general related prices to costs in a way that carries conviction.

Prices and costs

The convention that Comecon countries sell their exports to the market economies at local market prices has served to prevent disruption; but it has also kept down the level of trade. As in the case of Japan, followed by a number of small East Asian and Mediterranean countries, their lower wages should, by the logic of comparative costs, have been reflected in rapidly expanding exports of labour intensive products to the advanced industrial countries. The planners' internal policies of concentration on heavy industry and the system's neglect of the consumer contributed to the East European countries' failure to do this, but so also did the import policies of the West European countries, faced with the possibility of cheap imports the validity of whose prices they were unable to establish.

It seems likely that much potential trade will continue to be stillborn so long as prices in the directive economies are not believed to be a serious indicator of costs. International political relations may also be regarded as less satisfactory when the concept of fair trade is an arbitrary one, not verifiable by reference to principles of price formation accepted by both sides. The Comecon countries want to make prices reflect costs in a way that is mutually comprehensible and convincing among themselves. Will their efforts to do so succeed? And if they do, will the prices be comprehensible and convincing in the West too?

There are two causes of the differences between the price systems in market and directive economies: the methods by which prices are fixed, and the concepts according to which they are fixed. The differences of method may well be more important than those of concept.

Control over the prices of the several million articles that are produced in each economy is a very big job — too big, perhaps, for it to be properly done without using a ridiculous number of skilled people in the price control office. Even if the job could in theory be done by a reasonable number of people, there is the further difficulty that decisions by governments about prices are political decisions, affecting real incomes and raising strong passions, as the Polish authorities have good reason to know since the riots over price increases in 1970.

These administrative and political blockages have so far prevented the leaders of the directive economies from evolving systems of prices that they can use for their mutual trade; and the Hungarians chose to install the new economic mechanism in one radical step instead of as a series of little reforms because they thought this was the only way to escape the distortions of the administrative system.

The Hungarians do seem to have reformed their prices in this way so that they are a passable indicator of costs; and the other countries may decide to do the same, or may find that, contrary to the Hungarians' belief, they can reach the same result *ambulando*. Would it then be found that differences of concept still prevented comparisons of the price systems?

In the case of the Hungarians' guided market economy the GATT has implied that the prices are comparable with those of other market economies, in accepting Hungary as a contracting party without reservations relating to their price system. But are the concepts according to which prices in directive economies are formed necessarily different?

There can be two causes of difference: economic, because for example capital or land is priced differently, investments are decided on a different basis, or prices are put at average instead of marginal costs; and social, because products are differently taxed or subsidised on social grounds. Differences in the pricing of capital have been much reduced since the Comecon countries introduced interest rates. They still concentrate on having a high rate of investment, particularly in heavy industry. But the encouragement of a high rate of investment is not unknown in market economies; nor does it seem likely to cause a major distortion of prices. The difference between average and marginal costs may well be substantial, but it is calculable, so that account could be taken of it in fixing external trade prices.

Implicit subsidies/taxes on social grounds seem to be important in Comecon countries. The planners doubtless have much difficulty in getting expensive factories to reduce their costs or in closing them down. But such problems are hardly unknown in the West: in Britain, official subsidies to industries have been running at a level not far short of £1,000 million a year, and regional aids have been estimated to amount to 5−7½ per cent of total costs. It is not by accident that non-tariff distortions of trade are beginning to rival tariffs as a focus of attention in the GATT.

A logical solution to this problem within the GATT would be to require contracting parties to provide information as to the net size of the subsidies received by a given exporting sector or firm, and to authorise the country receiving these exports to levy a countervailing duty unless the exporting country imposes an export levy of equivalent amount. If the directive economies can arrive at convincingly rational calculations of their costs, a similar system could be applied in their trade with the market economies − even if the levies would be more numerous and on average of greater size than in the trade between market economies.

So long as the directive economies' prices remain as opaque as they now are, a general system of this sort could hardly be applied; but it might be possible to give special consideration to the costs of a limited number of products whose sales the Eastern exporter thought could be substantial if a lower price were allowed. If the case were made, the price could be reduced and sales expanded at a rate that gave the domestic industries in the Community adequate time to adjust. At the same time, the general question of price formation could be discussed between East and West in order to determine the conditions under which external trade prices could be dealt with by a more general system that related them to costs.

Discussions of these problems took place when East European countries applied to participate in the GATT. But they were not profound, nor did they take place with those that have not applied to join the GATT, most importantly the Soviet Union. It is suggested that the Community should allocate substantial resources to studies of the problems of price formation in Eastern and Western Europe, undertaken both by independent research centres and by its own officials, and should encourage discussions either in the ECE or directly with Comecon, which has been carrying out its own studies of prices.

At the same time, the Community should recognise the potential for improved trade relations with countries such as Hungary, which have adopted cost-related price systems, and should respond with favourable trade policies — for example, in the case of Hungary, by removing the quotas which have, under the protocol governing Hungarian accession to the GATT, been maintained despite the acceptance by the Community and other parties to the GATT that Hungary has a market economy.

Such measures on the part of the Community can be justified on plain business grounds. Trade will flourish better if both sides have mutually comprehensible and compatible price systems. In addition, there is a reasonable expectation, even though it cannot be confirmed by proof, that this would help towards the establishment of a more just and reliable international framework for economic relations.

Conclusion

Our search for Community economic policies towards Eastern Europe and the Soviet Union which, while valid in economic terms, would contribute to the Community's political objectives in East—West relations, has had some positive results.

The Community should be able to establish itself as a heavyweight economic partner of the Soviet Union by combining its members' industrial and financial resources to carry out big co-operation projects. It should also show its diplomatic efficacy by being ready to negotiate a multilateral set of principles for East—West trade which would recognise the existence of Comecon, followed by detailed trade negotiations between individual Comecon countries and the Community.

The Community would favour East European autonomy if it avoids making detailed arrangements that would increase supranational control over East European trade policies; if its trading and financial resources are available as a counterweight to the predominant power of the Soviet Union; and if it responds readily to moves in Eastern Europe towards more cost-reflecting price systems and market-oriented economic systems, for just as common interventions in Comecon imply detailed supranational constraint, so the replacement of directive by market mechanisms would reduce the scope of detailed constraint.

Similarly, the Community can encourage the development of more reliable and just international procedures and institutions in its economic relations with the East if its policies are responsive to those aspects of economic reforms in Eastern Europe that tend towards compatible price mechanisms and market systems; and it might open the way to more rational price relationships by promoting discussions on the issues of price in external trade, with respect to both the prices of specific products and the problems of relationships between different systems. The relationship may well suffer from a simple lack of understanding of some rather complex problems, and the Community should be ready to put money into the study of these problems.

To present its united strength to the Soviet Union and demonstrate the scale of resources that it can bring to bear in cooperation, the Community could announce the availability of finance from the European Investment Bank for big cooperation projects, and offer to negotiate cooperation as well as trade agreements with the Soviet Union or any East European country. The Community cooperation agreements would coexist with the member governments' own cooperation agreements with Eastern countries, the Community's agreements applying only to those projects too big for an individual member country to handle.

Such a pluralist system, with agreements made by both the Community and the member states, may seem peculiar to those who are steeped in the centralised traditions of government in Britain or France. It is however the system which operates for Community aid to developing countries, with the European Development Fund operating alongside the member governments' national aid programmes; and, internally, the Community has its anti-trust laws relating to activities that affect intra-Community trade alongside the member countries' own laws which govern activities affecting only their domestic economies.

The idea of an external policy that aims both to create or maintain a balance of power and to establish or strengthen international procedures and institutions with the same countries may also seem contradictory. But it responds to two distinct needs in the international system in general and in East—West relations in particular; and policy measures such as the coordination of resources for cooperation projects or the development of new systems to deal with price relationships between Eastern and Western economies can contribute to both types of objective — the classic and the modern — at the same time. The Community should be well placed to pursue both objectives, since the very fact of unity helps to redress the imbalance of power in Europe, while the method of its unity — the integration of economies of which none is in a position to dominate the others — gives it special experience of the processes whereby international procedures and institutions can be established between equal partners.

Notes

[1] The Community's activities up to 1972 are reviewed in Chapter 4 of Charles Ransom, *The Community and Eastern Europe,* Butterworths, London 1974.

[2] For example by Ernst B. Haas in *The Uniting of Europe,* Stevens, London 1958.

[3] In *Communist International Economics,* Blackwell, Oxford 1968.

[4] In *Coexistence and Commerce: Guidelines for Transactions between East and West,* McGraw-Hill, London 1970, Chapter 25.

[5] *Comprehensive Programme for the Further Extension and Improvement of Cooperation and the Development of Socialist Economic Integration by the CMEA Member-Countries,* CMEA Secretariat, Moscow, 1971.

[6] R. Selucky, *Economic Reforms in Eastern Europe: Political Background and Economic Significance,* Praeger Publishers, New York 1972.

[7] *Communication on Problems arising from Cooperation Agreements and Proposal for a Council Decision establishing a Consultation Procedure for Cooperation Agreements between Member States and Third Countries,* COM (73) 1275 final, 13 October 1973.

[8] In 'On the Economic Theory of Socialism', *Review of Economic Studies,* October 1936 and February 1937.

[9] See for example M. Kaser and J. Zielinski, *Planning in East Europe,* The Bodley Head, London 1970; and J. Wilczynski, *Profit, Risk and Incentives under Socialist Economic Planning,* The Macmillan Press Ltd., London, 1973.

[10] W. Brus, author of *The Market in a Socialist Economy,* Routledge and Kegan Paul, London 1972; and O. Sik, author of *Plan and Market under Socialism,* Academic Publishing House of the Czechoslovak Academy of Sciences, 1967.

[11] See Kaser and Zielinski, op.cit., and G. Denton, *A New Economic Mechanism?* PEP, London 1971.

[12] A number of them are summarised in J. Wilczynski, *Towards Multilateral Payments in Comecon Foreign Trade,* Occasional Paper no. 914, Committee for Economic Development of Australia, Sydney, 1971.

[13] *Comprehensive Programme,* op.cit.

[14] Op.cit., Section 6.28.

[15] Op.cit., Section 7.16.

[16] Op.cit., Section 7.18.

[17] Op.cit., Section 7.16.

[18] Op.cit., Section 7.5.

6   Defence Collaboration in the European Community

J.C. GARNETT

This chapter is a revised version of a paper first presented at a seminar held at the National Defence College and later published in J.G. Garnett (ed.), *The Defence of Western Europe*, Macmillan, London 1974.

This chapter is orientated towards the future rather than the past, but it contains no predictions and it cannot fairly be described as 'futurology'. At best it is a piece of plausible political speculation, a fumbling exploration of what might be, which is rooted in the author's perception of recent trends in European politics. Discussion is concentrated on the prospects for greater Community collaboration in defence, the most politically sensitive and jealously guarded of all government activities. Much of it was written before the 1973 energy crisis, and if it was an ambitious subject then, when the Community seemed relatively prosperous, it must surely seem even more ambitious today, when the Community is in disarray and very much on the defensive. At a time when most of its supporters are trying to preserve what has already been achieved it may be an inopportune moment to look ahead towards the final stages in creating a European identity.

But it is far too early to say whether progress towards European union has now ground to a permanent halt or whether it has merely received a temporary setback. Europe is still very much a society of sovereign states but there are modest signs that the Community is emerging as an international actor in its own right, with an identity over and above that of its members. The fact that the Community was able to present a common position with respect to the Conference on Security and Cooperation in Europe is an example of the significant progress made in this direction. And at the Copenhagen summit of December 1973, members affirmed their determination to establish the Community as a 'distinct and original entity'. The foreign ministers were convinced that 'Europe must write and speak increasingly with a single voice if it wants to make itself heard and play its proper role in the world'. Of course no one should make too much of what has been achieved. Certainly it is not yet clear that in speaking of the Community we should talk of 'it' rather than a plurality of members, or, to use Andrew Shonfield's phrases 'a melting pot' rather than 'a bag of marbles'.[1]

But if we assume for a moment that progress will continue to be made, slowly and then inevitably as the Community interests itself in political matters, questions of defence collaboration are bound to arise. Indeed, even if there is no further progress towards a united Europe, questions relating to cooperation in the defence field are likely to be raised. It is surely worthwhile to consider this area of activity even if it is not of immediate concern to decision makers in Brussels.

Unfortunately collaboration in the field of defence cannot be considered in isolation from the more general and fundamental problem of foreign policy coordination. After all, defence policy is the handmaiden of foreign policy. It provides the military power to implement foreign policy objectives, and if it is taken out of this political context it makes very little sense. Unless the nine members of the EEC can agree on a common foreign policy, it is virtually impossible for them to agree on a common defence policy, though they may still agree to cooperate further in the defence field. The first part of this chapter must, therefore, speculate about the Community's international identity and its role in the world.

Whatever role is finally adopted, Western European statesmen are bound to find their choices severely circumscribed by the attitudes and policies of the many states with whom they will have to deal. Antony Hartley is probably right in his suggestion that 'a political Europe beginning to emerge in the late seventies will be liable to discover its freedom of action limited by international decisions in which it has had no say and which its component parts have been too weak to affect'.[2] In particular, the freedom of Europe to shape its own destiny may be seriously undermined both by the policies of the superpowers and by the rise of non-European states to positions of power and influence in world affairs. However unpalatable it might have been to such old-fashioned nationalists as de Gaulle, Europe is no longer the cockpit of the world, and her future will be determined by decisions taken outside Europe as well as those in Europe. So far as Europe's future is concerned, Senator Mansfield is at least as important as Chancellor Schmidt and President Giscard d'Estaing, and few would doubt that Mr Ford and Mr Kosygin are more important than both of them.

The respective policies of the two superpowers towards Europe impose very obvious constraints on the freedom of European states, either individually or collectively, to pursue their interests. What is not so obvious is that the European policies of both the Soviet Union and the

United States are very much influenced by their relationship with each other. It is for this reason that détente — always likely to develop into an exclusive, bilateral superpower relationship — has always been a mixed blessing for Europe. So long as the USA and the Soviet Union continue to allocate the highest priority to improving their relationship with each other, European interests are bound to look vulnerable and European politicians are bound to feel uneasy. Indeed suspicion, however vague and unjustified, of superpower collusion if not condominium, will provide a very real motive for European unity if it transpires that the Soviets and the Americans are prepared to ride roughshod over European interests. As the superpowers become reluctant to jeopardise the détente which has sprung up between them for the sake of purely European interests, the European states may find that only those policies which do not involve the superpowers in any risks can command acceptance, let alone positive support.

It may sound a little fanciful — though de Gaulle did not think so — to speculate on the nightmare possibility of positive American–Soviet cooperation or collusion at the expense of Europe. But it is certainly true that the combined pressure and influence of the two superpowers could make savage inroads into Europe's freedom to manoeuvre. Even without any malevolent cooperation, the superpowers wield enormous, perhaps decisive, power in European affairs. And it is surely fair to suggest that a developing Europe must not count either on the continuing passivity of the Soviet Union or the continuing benevolence of the United States towards European integration.

The Soviet Union has never looked with equanimity upon the emergence of a resurgent Europe. The prospect of a powerful and possibly hostile superpower on their western as well as eastern frontiers is a daunting proposition for Soviet leaders, and it is not surprising, therefore, that Soviet hostility towards all attempts at European integration, including the Common Market, has been a consistent feature of their diplomacy. Although they may have relinquished any ideas of territorial conquest in Western Europe, the Soviets recognise that only by keeping Europe divided and weak can they hope to exercise preponderant influence. There is no need to suppose that the Soviets will take physical steps to prevent the emergence of a powerful Western Europe, even one with a European Defence Community of some sort, but it seems fair to assume that whatever progress is made in this direction will be without their help and, indeed, in spite of considerable diplomatic opposition.

Needless to say, Soviet hostility to the idea of a Europe which is integrated militarily as well as economically should not be used as an argument for not pressing ahead with it. European states are not yet so overshadowed by their superpower neighbour that policies have to be tailored to please it. No doubt the Soviets will wax eloquent on the subject of German militarism and American imperialism, but in effect moves towards European defence integration are unlikely to cause more than a ripple on the smooth waters of détente. After all, as François Duchêne has pointed out, there is nothing provocative about improving one's minimum security arrangements.[3]

The attitude of the USA is a good deal more equivocal. Traditionally, the USA has enthusiastically supported the idea of European integration and independence. Successive Presidents have extolled the virtues of a new and independent centre of power able and willing to act in harmony with the USA and to shoulder worldwide responsibilities. President Kennedy's 'twin pillar' idea of Atlantic partnership reflected this persistent strand in American foreign policy, and as recently as 1971 President Nixon reaffirmed his support for the idea: 'The United States has always supported the strengthening and enlargement of the European Community. We still do. We welcome cohesion in Europe because it makes Europe a sturdier pillar of the structure of peace.'[4]

It may be too cynical to suggest that some American proponents of European unity see a successful political and military entity on this side of the Atlantic as a good excuse for sliding out of their NATO commitments. But it is certainly true that an improved level of competence and effort in the European part of NATO would make it easier for the USA to press ahead with its planned withdrawals. Once again, this should not be used as ammunition against European defence integration. Whether the Europeans sort themselves out or not, the USA is likely to reduce its commitment. Prolonging Europe's weakness is unlikely to delay the process, and conceivably, by irritating the Americans, may actually hasten it.

But the real implications of a united Europe have only recently been thought through in the USA. Very few supporters of European unity seemed to realise that even a potential superpower would be more difficult to manage than a divided conglomeration of independent sovereign states, and even fewer contemplated the very real possibility that the interests of a united Europe might well diverge sharply from those of the USA. Some of these possibilities are now keenly appreciated in Washington, and although officially the government is still well disposed towards the idea of a united Europe, the idea of 'partnership' has a hollow ring to it and there are plenty of signs of diminishing enthusiasm.

Many Americans are openly worried about the policies which an inward-looking, introspective Europe might follow, and they have been particularly agitated by the policies of trade discrimination of the EEC. Obviously, the development of a unitary, preferential trading bloc comprising most of Western Europe and linked by preferential trade agreements to Africa and the Mediterranean could have serious consequences for the American economy. The American Government has already reacted quite sharply, and it is clear that the future will see some very hard bargaining over a whole range of trade problems. It is reasonable to suppose that as the economic costs of supporting Europe impinge more heavily on the American economy, the government may find it increasingly difficult to justify its political support for European unity. A slightly worsening trade relationship might be regarded as a fair price to pay for the achievement of more important political goals, but when even these are being questioned, criticism is inevitable. It is difficult to avoid R. Cooper's[5] conclusion that although the USA has supported the unification of Europe, including Britain, for the past quarter century, dispassionate analysis may question the wisdom of this position for the last half of that period.

It is arguable that the international implications inherent in a united Europe are even more profound than is generally appreciated either in the Soviet Union or the USA. A great deal will depend upon the kind of Europe which develops. Joining the European Community is a bit like stepping on an escalator travelling at variable speed towards an unknown but, it is hoped, desirable destination. So far political scientists have not reflected very much on the nature of a united Europe. They have accepted unity as a self-evidently virtuous goal and they have been too obsessed by the problems of bringing it about to think very much about how it might behave.

It may be that the Europe which emerges will be a 'low profile' Europe, fairly introspective and content to jog along between the superpowers and in uneasy partnership with one of them. But a much more assertive Europe is a long term possibility which cannot be ignored. Indeed, the political will and energy which are required to unite Europe in the first place are precisely the qualities likely to push her into an active and positive world role. Western Europe is already one of the wealthiest pieces of real estate in the world. The Community of Nine will have a combined GNP of over £250,000 million, and a very high level of industrial development. Militarily speaking it can muster more than two million men under arms, some strategic nuclear capability, powerful air forces and, apart from the superpowers, the strongest naval forces in the world. Potentially, Western Europe is in the superpower league, and if unity should fire her ambition, her influence and importance could be enormous. The development of a 'third force' Europe, anxious to engage in the traditional game of power politics and equipped with nuclear weapons and superpower confidence and ambition, could not fail to have the most profound effects on global strategy and the pattern of world politics. It is idle to suppose that the emergence of such a superstate would be regarded with either equanimity or approval in many parts of the world.

Superpower Europe, a vast regional bloc, playing, on a grand scale, the age-old game of nation states, is not what the original architects of the European Community had in mind. And there are many Europeans who feel uneasy about such a role. They would prefer a more obviously virtuous Europe, probably a non-nuclear Europe, outward looking in the sense of showing proper concern for the development of the Third World, but not outward looking in the sense of being willing to acquire and use military power in the pursuit of its interests around the world. Whether, in a society of independent sovereign states, a militarily castrated Europe makes political sense is doubtful. Traditionally most states, even neutrals, have found the possession of military power an indispensable instrument of survival in a world which, if not hostile, is frequently apathetic towards the fate of those who cannot fend for themselves.

But 'Great Power Europe', militarily on the same footing as the superpowers, is, if it is possible at all, in the distant future. In terms of practical politics, Europe is now, and is likely to remain in the foreseeable future, dependent on the USA for strategic and conventional military power. Although, as a result of the present reappraisal, the American–European relationship is likely to undergo some readjustment, Europe's dependence is likely to continue to be one of the most important constraints on her freedom to manoeuvre. While it exists it is impossible to think of Europe pursuing policies with which the USA seriously disagrees. There is therefore no question of Europe acting independently of her major ally, and no question of dismantling the major alliance which links them.

NATO is the cornerstone of Western defence, and though one may look forward to the development within NATO of a consciously European caucus, the alliance will continue to provide the major institutional framework for the operational aspects of European defence. The Community's growing interest in foreign and defence policy need not undermine the alliance's fundamental role in Europe, though it may lead to developments within the alliance which will help put the European–American relationship on a steadier and more balanced footing. The 1973 December Summit held in Copenhagen did a little to spell out the

Community view of European—American defence relations. Members of the Community asserted their wish to preserve its 'mutually beneficial' ties with the USA. They declared that 'under the present circumstances, there is no alternative to the security provided by the nuclear weapons of the United States and by the presence of North American troops in Europe'.[6] By this statement the Community explicitly accepted the Atlantic basis, though not necessarily the NATO basis, of European defence.

The precise nature of united Europe is not yet clear, but there is mounting evidence that it will not be one in which there are strong and powerful supranational institutions. The supranational, Monnetist philosophy which was so popular in the early years has taken some hard knocks from contemporary politicians — particularly in Britain and France where there is widespread fear of a Europe characterised by institutional dogmatism and illiberal bureaucracy. Mr Heath reassured a good many people when, in reporting his conversations with M. Pompidou in May 1971, he spoke of their agreement that 'the identity of national states should be maintained in the framework of the developing community ... the processes of harmonisation should not override essential national interests'.

Mr Heath's 'minimalist' pragmatic vision of European unity was elaborated in his 1967 Godkin Lectures at Harvard, but in some ways it was an ambiguous and unsatisfactory conception. On the one hand he was clearly unwilling to contemplate a straight federal solution, a unitary European state with superpower potential, but on the other hand he appeared to recognise that the Community was not just another cooperative association of independent sovereign states.[7] Mr Heath spoke enthusiastically about the idea of Community involvement in the fields of foreign policy and defence, and he quoted with approval Robert Menzies' comment that 'a customs union cannot stand still and has no alternative but to go forward to democratic control or back to national systems'.[8] The then Prime Minister obviously recognised that the EEC was a political reality of a quite different order to, say, NATO. As Leonard Beaton has noted,[9] Mr Heath seemed to be advocating an entirely new political animal, an institutional arrangement which goes far deeper than NATO or any existing cooperative association, but which stops short of being a state. Whether such an institution makes either practical or even theoretical sense as a permanent goal is rather doubtful, though as a transitional phase it can clearly be defended.

The Common Market has already acquired certain, albeit weak, supranational features. In the Council of Ministers, for example, there is already a system of qualified majority voting. And the Commission, which represents the Community as a whole, is, because of its independent role as initiator of Community policy, defender of Community interests and executor of Community decisions, a qualitatively different kind of body from traditional international secretariats. The European states have already created political institutions which limit their sovereign independence.

However, although the sovereignty issue is at the heart of European Community politics, it is easy to make too much of it. In the modern world, powers of medium size, even though they retain the formal apparatus of sovereignty, have already lost a good deal of their scope for practical political choice. Forces external to the state are circumscribing the freedom of all but the most powerful, and sovereignty in the practical sense of freedom to determine one's destiny, as opposed to the legal sense, is already deeply eroded. Joining the Common Market simply means having rather less of something which no one has very much of anyway.

It is almost certainly an illusion to believe that in a developing European Community critical decision making power can remain a monopoly of national governments. Even a purely economic community is really a political phenomenon. Walter Hallstein was almost right when he said: 'We are not in business, we are in politics'. [10] In reality the two cannot be separated. Though some politicians may delude themselves, the gradual reshaping of economic relations between member countries is a process which inexorably whittles away their sovereign independence until, almost without anyone realising it, a point is reached when independent action becomes a physical impossibility, and sovereignty a complete fiction. David Mitrany was one of the first to see the significance of this. His so-called 'functional approach' to integration avoided the politically sensitive issue of sovereignty by concentrating on limited, practical arrangements which undermine sovereign independence without ever raising the issue. [11] Mr Heath's essentially Gaullist idea of a 'Europe of states' did not avoid the problem of sovereignty; it merely avoided making a political issue of it until it was too late to do anything about it. What will happen in the case of the European Community is that although individual members will retain actual and legal control over their instruments of policy, they will discover that these instruments lose their effectiveness. States will find themselves able to pursue their objectives, but quite unable to achieve them. To take an extreme case, as the Europeans become more mixed up in each others' economic, military and political affairs, as national economies become more unbalanced and as joint defence projects proliferate, it is possible to imagine a situation in which individual European states which have retained their freedom to declare war find, when the crunch comes, that they are unable to wage it simply because they have become inextricably involved with partners who are now unwilling to support them.

The gist of the argument so far has been to suggest that, while there may be no immediate defence implication for the enlarged European Community, and as the members become increasingly involved in each others' material interests and affairs, they will create a community of needs and interests which have very real defence and foreign policy implications. As David Owen recently put it, 'On any rational basis it is inconceivable that, in the long term, defence will be excluded from the movement towards European integration . . .'[12]

After all, it is quite inconsistent to aim, on the one hand, at a Common Market with the fullest possible division of labour on a continental scale, and on the other hand to pour money and research into purely national defence programmes. The national and independent control of defence is frequently regarded as the ultimate symbol of sovereignty, but the sheer waste in terms of duplicated effort and misallocated resources makes this one of the most expensive myths of our time. The separation of defence from other aspects of economic planning has already led to a very artificial — and expensive — dichotomy between civil and military research. On the civil side the Common Market is already involved in planning and funding a long list of high-technology projects, some of which will involve work which overlaps essential research in the defence field. Somehow, in the interests of economy, ways must be found for merging under the same authority all high-technology research for both civil and military projects.[13]

A fully fledged European Defence Community (EDC) to complement the Common Market is a logical, if somewhat ambitious, goal, and its virtues are considerable. It could ensure the most effective collective use of national resources to provide a well equipped and balanced European Army, backed, if necessary, by strategic nuclear capability of some significance. It could encourage member states to 'unbalance' their national forces in the interests of efficiency and specialisation. It could produce a unified European strategic posture and by ironing out differences in tactical doctrine it could enable European forces to be deployed across national frontiers to the best possible defensive positions. It could organise the rationalisation of defence procurement on an international basis, enforce standardisation in weaponry and equipment, improve logistics, and in every respect enable the European to get value for money in the defence field. By rationally exploiting the very considerable defence effort of nine European states, a powerful EDC could make Europe a genuine centre of power and a counterbalance to American power in NATO. Inevitably, an EDC voice would carry a good deal of weight not just in NATO, but in the world at large.

However, as was hinted at the beginning of this chapter, it would be quite wrong to believe that the Community is now set upon a course which will lead swiftly and inevitably to the creation of a Defence Community. At the moment there are few signs that members are successfully forging a common foreign policy, and yet this is surely a vital prerequisite for any fully fledged EDC. In the words of Lord Balniel, 'Fully effective defence collaboration must depend on the merging and harmonisation of wider political aims'.[13]

The obstacles to a unified foreign policy are formidable and they are exemplified by recent French policy. The French have consistently pursued policies which are particularly difficult to reconcile with the creation of a Community foreign policy. It remains to be seen how far post-Gaullist politicians in France will break away from the Gaullist philosophy of M. Debré and the late President Pompidou. Certainly it is impossible to reconcile either a common foreign policy or an EDC with Debré's denial of any European identity, and his comment that 'life throughout the world is based, and will be based in coming years, upon nation states, and the foundation of all security for men, women, and their homes will be the political and military ability of the nation states to guarantee, in so far as that is possible, their security'.[14] Though not so well articulated in other European countries, this kind of reasoning has a fairly wide appeal and the sentiments and feeling on which it is based constitute a formidable, if not insurmountable, obstacle to any unified foreign or defence policy.

Even before the energy crisis and the ensuing bitterness between Community members, there were plenty of signs that the Community had lost much of its momentum towards full political union; but it was the Arabs' oil policy announced in the autumn of 1973 which provided an acid test of precisely how much progress the Davignon Committee had made towards coordinating foreign policies. It was quite embarrassing to see how the Dutch call for 'Community solidarity' went unheeded, and how the British and French not only refused to contemplate policies likely to undermine their status as 'friendly' nations, but actually pursued bilateral initiatives to secure privileged access to oil supplies.

Some of the wounds inflicted at that time are now healing, but in spite of Mr Tickell's optimistic comments about the Community's united front at the Conference on Security and Cooperation in Europe,[15] it would be dangerous to conclude that members are now hammering out a common foreign policy on the many issues which face them. Hedley Bull's comment that 'in international politics outside Europe the countries of Western Europe have no common policy' [16] is still valid. The search for a European identity is in its infancy, and there is much truth in Mr Alting von Geusau's gloomy description of the Community 'not as a new actor in international relations, but as a sub-system in permanent crisis over its external relations and internal development'.[17]

In the light of this political fragmentation and lack of common purpose it is difficult to see how any European Defence Community could either operate or even be brought into existence.

The difficulties of creating a European Defence Community are exacerbated by the fact in the defence field it is impossible to start from scratch. Those who planned and created the European Economic Community did not have to compete with an existing customs union; they started with a clean slate. But in the defence field a new organisation would enjoy no comparable advantage. It would have to develop alongside existing defence arrangements which are well established and which cannot be easily dismantled or incorporated in a new set-up. The European web of complex, if untidy, defence arrangements is dominated by NATO and its militarily active members. Within it, but not of it, is the recently created Euro Group which facilitates multilateral defence cooperation at a very practical level between its ten members. A slightly different net is provided by the Western European Union (WEU), which has seven members (including France) and a residual number of defence and arms control functions. In addition to these formal structures there is an elaborate network of bilateral cooperation at the military and politico-military levels. In Europe there is already a considerable corpus of collaborative experience in practical defence consultations which some would argue ought not to be unduly disturbed by the creation of yet another organisation in the same line of business. If a new defence organisation is required it ought, perhaps, to arise out of this evolutionary process which has already acquired the kind of momentum which can be halted only by conscious political decisions.

And there are very real practical difficulties in replacing Europe's rather complicated defence arrangements by a single, coherent system. Undertaking any major structural alterations with a family in residence is inevitably a messy and difficult business. In this particular case, sensible alterations and tidy planning are made even more difficult by awkward relatives. There is, for example, a rich and powerful uncle who has to be accommodated because his continuing support is essential to the family's wellbeing for a number of years. And there is an even more obstreperous relative who, in any planned refurbishing, has to be provided for even though for the moment he insists on maintaining his own establishment. Equally awkward are those less close relatives who, on commonsense grounds, might more appropriately be accommodated in adjacent cottages but who still insist on remaining under the parental roof.

The very real difficulties of accommodating diverse interests within a single grouping have led some to speculate about the possibility of a defence organisation — perhaps a modified WEU — which was concerned primarily with the problems associated with the Central Front. At least two comments, one general and one specific, are possible. First, it is worth pointing out that effective collaboration in an alliance does not require, as the critics imply, an identity of interests between the members. All that is necessary is that each partner should see an advantage in cooperating. The fact that they do not see the same advantage does not matter. Hence quite diverse states may, for diverse reasons and in the pursuit of diverse interests, cooperate. Second, it is difficult to imagine WEU, with its aura of failure, as a revitalised organisation. And from the British point of view, if it was rejuvenated it would be dangerous to assume that Britain could dominate it. On certain plausible growth projections, it may be that by 1980 both France and the Federal Republic will be half as rich again as Britain. In collaboration with such strong partners the British might find themselves in the back seat.

However, in spite of the difficulties, one may expect the enlargement of the Community to give a further fillip to the integration movement among its members, if only because other international developments are pushing the Europeans in the same direction. And since the enlarged Community includes Britain, France and the Federal Republic — the three most significant military powers in Europe — one might expect their collaborative ventures to be important.

One of the most insistent outside pressures on the Europeans to cooperate in the defence field comes, paradoxically, from the Soviet Union. The residual Soviet threat is sufficiently well appreciated to encourage the West Europeans to improve their cooperative efforts in the security field. [18] In spite of détente, perceptive Europeans have noted that, at the very moment when the USA is tiring of its world role and reducing its overseas involvements, the Soviet Union is becoming interested in playing a global role and is already acquiring the military capability to make it effective. Growing naval strength in the Mediterranean and the continuous, if unspectacular, improvements in Warsaw Pact forces are two clear indications of the way in which the military balance in Europe is shifting against the West.

So long as the Soviet Union remains ideologically committed to revolutionary change and sufficiently powerful to look as if she might be tempted to try her luck, European states are bound to feel the need to protect themselves. The Soviet threat is real, though more ambiguous than it used to be, and most thoughtful Europeans recognise that the kind of sustained military effort which is required to counter it can most painlessly be achieved on a cooperative, 'European' basis.

Of the numerous political and economic pressures which are encouraging collaboration in the defence field, the most significant is the very real prospect of American withdrawal from the continent they have defended for so long. Of course, President Nixon has emphasised the abiding and undiminished commitment of the USA to defend Western Europe: 'In the third decade of our commitment to Europe, the depth of our relationship is a fact of life. We can no more disengage from Europe than from Alaska'. [19] But the term 'commitment' is ambiguous and can be misleading. In the context of American–European relations it may refer either to a legally binding promise by the USA to provide assistance to Western Europe in the event of Soviet aggression, or to an abiding physical peacetime presence in Europe which takes the form of stationing men and equipment in the European theatre. The American commitment in the former sense is unquestioned, but in the latter sense there is plenty of evidence that it is likely to diminish. Although the Mansfield Resolution was defeated, the mood which it sprang from is likely to remain a vocal and peaceful pressure in American politics. The Nixon doctrine and the talk about a more genuine partnership and 'burden-sharing' are the firm indications that the American military involvement in Europe is likely to change from preponderance to inferiority.

The creation of a Euro Group in NATO, and initiatives such as the European Defence Improvement Programme, may be regarded as the first, tentative European reactions to ex-President Nixon's firm and entirely reasonable insistence that Europe undertake a fair share of its own defence. It seems sensible to suppose that in the face of American troop withdrawals and a diminution of effort, the Europeans will be forced to make good the deficiencies in their defence posture. However, though the argument is unassailable in logic, it is by no means cast iron. European politicians may find it politically convenient to believe that if the Americans feel it is safe enough to withdraw, then the threat of Soviet invasion, already fairly incredible to many of them, must be sufficiently near zero to need no increased defence effort. Even those who recognise the threat may be tempted to ignore it on the grounds that Western

Europe is incapable of dealing with it without crippling herself economically. The argument is that if we in Europe are condemned to living
dangerously whatever we do, then we might as well live cheaply as well. In
an atmosphere of détente in which every government in Western Europe is
trying to reduce its defence expenditure, there are enormous pressures to
see it this way. If, however, increased effort is deemed necessary, then
increased cooperation in the defence field will seem an attractive way for
individual states to minimise their financial burdens. In the end, the very
selfish motive of saving money may be the most important pressure
towards collaboration, even integration, in the defence field.

There is a depressing intractability about defence economics which may
force the states of Europe into reluctant cooperation. The British
experience is as relevant as any. At a time when the cost of building a
frigate is about 75 per cent higher than it was in the late 1950s, and the
capital cost of an armoured regiment equipped with Chieftains about 80
per cent higher than the cost of one equipped with Centurions, the British
have reduced the proportion of their GNP spent on defence from about 8
per cent to just over 5 per cent. It seems reasonable to expect that, once
inside the Common Market, in order not to be economically dis-
advantaged, Britain will not allow its defence expenditure to exceed the
average of its European partners. This would imply that by the end of the
decade, and in spite of costs rising more quickly than GNP, Britain will be
spending less than 4 per cent of its GNP on defence. This is not as much as
it − or other European states − can afford, but given the prevailing
political climate, it is as much as anyone is prepared to pay.

At this level of effort, it is unlikely that even the larger states of
Western Europe will be able to maintain their traditional spectrum of
military power. Trying to do too much with too little is a certain recipe
for doing nothing effectively. It may be that only by specialising, by
deliberately unbalancing their forces, will European states be able to
achieve a credible defence posture in any area. If they can coordinate their
'unbalancing' policies, West European states might avoid dangerous gaps in
their collective defence posture and make significant savings. The
argument is that by unbalancing their national forces, the European states
will provide properly 'balanced' forces for an entity which is much more
powerful than all of them put together. Putting it simply, the Europeans
will be able either to maintain existing levels of military strength for less
money or improve them for the same amount.

This sort of military functionalism presupposes a certain degree of
harmony in strategic and tactical doctrine, and a good deal of trust in
allies, but as economic pressures mount, it is a pattern of behaviour which

European states will find difficult to resist. It should be clear, however, that this kind of specialisation would create very serious personnel problems within the armed forces, and is quite alien to our traditional way of thinking about defence. Moreover, it would be a political hot potato in the sense that participating countries would be consciously and deliberately allocating to their allies full responsibility for important aspects of their own defence. If it happened it would signify a commitment to Europe beside which the present assignment and earmarking of forces to NATO appears quite trivial. Timothy Stanley is probably right in his view that 'it is not in the present political cards to rationalise the division of labour so that one country concentrates on naval forces, another on air forces and so on', [20] but some sort of specialisation is probably inevitable.

There is no need to take the argument to the point where each state provides only one kind of military power. Even some degree of specialisation within the three services would bring considerable benefits. It is quite ridiculous, for example, that a small air force such as the one possessed by the Belgians should attempt the entire spectrum of roles implied by air defence, conventional bombing, nuclear bombing, close support, reconnaissance and anti-submarine. This kind of national diversification which leads even small states to try to do everything is a very inefficient use of resources.

The major argument against specialisation revolves around the possibility that a state may defect from mutually agreed arrangements, thereby leaving its allies exposed and vulnerable in certain categories of weaponry. If, for example, there had been this kind of specialisation within NATO during the first fifteen years of its life, the French withdrawal in 1967 might have had devastating implications for Western security. And in the context of specialisation it may be worth noting that from the British point of view a whole series of commitments outside Europe makes it that much more difficult for the British Government to relinquish certain kinds of capability to her NATO allies.

Already, but in a haphazard and therefore dangerous fashion, the smaller European states have found it necessary to specialise. The Belgian Navy, for example, has concentrated on a minesweeping role, and the Norwegian Navy on a coastal role with no deep sea capability. The Germans have relinquished their nuclear ambitions, and their air force has never attempted to acquire deep penetration capacity. It would be dangerous to read too much into the *ad hoc,* unilaterally decided specialisation that has gone on so far. After all, there is all the difference in the world between accepting a position of dependence and inadequacy which arises, as it were, out of the natural order of things, and positively organising such a state of affairs by making it official government policy. Nevertheless, in the long run systematic rationalisation along functional lines may be one way in which Western Europe can maintain a viable defence effort within the budgetary ceilings which are available. These days, money is the key to most decisions in the defence business, and ironically, though a united Europe has been the lofty aspiration of idealists motivated by the noblest sentiments, it may very well turn out that human greed and an obsession with material prosperity are the driving forces which turn aspiration into reality.

The economic and, for those who see it that way, the political advantages of going it with others in the defence field are available across the entire spectrum of weaponry. Not surprisingly, therefore, the pressure upon France and Britain, the only European nuclear powers, to cooperate in nuclear matters is formidable. The financial advantage to both parties would be considerable, and if the joint nuclear force was regarded as the primitive basis of a European deterrent, the political significance is undeniable, although it is debatable whether an Anglo–French force 'held in trust' would help unify Europe or whether it would create a nuclear élite which would divide Europe.

The problems of going it alone can be put quite simply. In the case of the French, the acquisition of nuclear capacity, even if it is of dubious effectiveness, is imposing a very heavy burden on the defence budget, and as Soviet defence systems become more sophisticated, it is unlikely that the French effort will diminish. During the third military plan from 1971 to 1975 it is estimated that one third of the £7,200 million to be spent on weapon procurement will be for nuclear arms. [21] Already the French spend more on their strategic forces than on any of the three services. The 1972 defence budget allocates £372 million or 27·5 per cent of the total to the nuclear deterrent. [22] It is possible that this figure will reduce to about 20 per cent by 1975, but this will be about ten times the British figure at that time. [23] As Ian Smart says, France is facing a great and increasing economic burden, the scale of which threatens to force the French Government to choose whether to increase its defence budget as a whole or to persist in penalising programmes for the re-equipment of the armed forces with modern conventional weapons. [24]

In the case of Britain, where the problem is one of perpetuating the usefulness of ageing systems and, in the long run, of replacing them with a new generation of weaponry, the financial burden is not so immediately onerous, but it is likely to increase very sharply indeed if Britain wishes to retain a viable deterrent in the 1980s and beyond. Hardening warheads and fitting MIRVs is an expensive business, and if the British decide to move to the next generation of delivery vehicles — probably ULMS, an Underwater Long Range Missile System — the costs will be astronomical. On balance it would seem that, of the two states, France is the more likely to be able to pursue an independent nuclear policy in the long run, but even she may fail in the end.

The choices available to both states are limited. Each can either cooperate with the USA, continue independently, cooperate with each other, or allow the present forces to 'rust out' without replacement. The French are unlikely to give up or to cooperate with the USA. The British, though they may go it alone in the short run, are quite likely to give up if they cannot cooperate with either the USA or France, or, ideally, both. For all sorts of reasons, political, technical and economic, some kind of Anglo—French cooperation seems desirable, but the obstacles are very real. Cooperation is hampered by British integration in NATO, by the nuclear relationship between Britain and the USA and the restrictive policies inherent in that association, by the suspicions and uneasiness of the Soviet Union, the USA and some European states, and, not least, by the Gaullist philosophy which, though crumbling around the edges, still dominates French policy. And there are very large question marks over the kind of cooperation which is possible. The French appear to want mainly technical and economic cooperation which would enable them to improve their own forces. They are very hostile to ideas of cooperation in any operational sense and seek mainly to promote national ambitions through collective effort. The British too are aware of the advantages of independent control, but the government tends to place more emphasis on the political, 'Europe building' role of cooperative effort.

Ideally, nuclear cooperation should follow rather than precede political integration, but time may not permit this. Military capability takes years to acquire, and unless cooperation is initiated in the near future, neither Britain, nor France, nor Europe will have any strategic nuclear forces after the present generation of weapons. The technologies involved in the nuclear weapons industry are so sophisticated that, once halted, it is doubtful if they could be picked up again even by a politically united Europe. The protracted timetable of weapon developments imparts a very special urgency to the question of Anglo—French nuclear cooperation, but there can be no confidence that the states involved will be able to overcome the difficulties.

Of course, attempts to collaborate in the defence field need not be as ambitious as those so far discussed. A European Defence Community is best regarded as the ultimate goal of a fully integrated European Community. A jointly owned, controlled and operated nuclear force is a

109

similarly ambitious scheme. Even arrangements for 'unbalancing' national forces to provide a 'balanced' European force must be regarded as a medium term goal still some years away. Perhaps the most immediately rewarding areas for defence collaboration between members of the European Community are the fields of weapon procurement and standardisation of equipment.

Collaboration over military equipment poses fewer political problems than more ambitious schemes, and in the context of current financial pressures, is beginning to be seen as a necessary way of making better use of the limited resources available for defence purposes. Some have suggested creating a European Common Market in defence equipment, with inducements to collaborate in procurement and constraints to discourage offshore purchase. Others favour the creation of an autonomous European Defence Procurement Agency responsible to European ministers for taking the initiative in promoting common procurement. R. Foch[25] has suggested a European Armaments Agency to define the needs of European countries for new armaments and to organise and finance the necessary research, development and industrial production for the equipment of European defence — at least in the conventional field. This proposal is not very different from A. Buchan's[26] idea of a European Advanced Project Authority designed to assure a Europe-wide market for expensive defence products by getting prior agreement on requirements, by spreading the cost of research, and by organising development and production wherever the most effective facilities exist. And it also has something in common with F. Duchêne's[27] notion of a European Defence Support Organisation with an interest in procurement, training and logistics.

Hugh Green has highlighted very serious practical problems in implementing some of these ideas. [28] He favours a modest continuation of the present voluntary approach to collaboration 'in which countries remain free to seek partners where they can find them.'[29] Green points out that in 1972 the Euro Group ministers agreed on a set of principles for equipment collaboration, the governing theme of which was the avoidance of unnecessary duplication. The Euro Group members undertook to consult and inform each other of the timing and content of plans for future military equipment, and they expressed determination to explore all possibilities of harmonising their policies. Ministers identified areas of possible collaboration and drew up guidelines for action within the Euro Group framework. Already some progress has been made in agreeing on the technical requirements for battlefield communication equipment which will ensure the complete interoperability of new systems as they come into service.

Modest cooperation based on the Euro Group has the very considerable virtue of political practicability, but no one should be under an illusion that it is more than an incremental step forward along the long road to a fully fledged European Defence Community. Indeed, in so far as it stresses cooperation between the states of Europe rather than integration it may actually postpone the kind of political initiatives which in the long run are necessary to transform the 'bag of marbles' into 'a melting pot'.

What is clear is that the pace of defence collaboration is intimately connected with the Community's more general progress towards a united Europe, and it seems probable that this pace is likely to be slower than might have been expected a year or two ago. With Britain inside the Community – at least for the time being – and with Gaullism on the wane, it did seem possible that the late 1970s would see the Community forge ahead after a period of stagnation. But at the moment there are no signs of that happening. However, although many Europeans may be quietly giving up the belief that the Community would rapidly lead them to a unified continental bloc comparable to that of the two superpowers, this need not force them to abandon every shred of European identity and every collaborative venture on the defence field. Indeed, they must expand their time scale and, in the short run at least, settle for more modest goals.

Notes

[1] A. Shonfield, *Europe: Journey to an Unknown Destination,* Penguin Books, London 1973, pp. 9–22.

[2] A. Hartley, 'Europe between the Super-Powers', *Foreign Affairs,* vol. XLIX, no. 2, January 1971, p. 272.

[3] F. Duchêne, 'A New European Defence Community', *Foreign Affairs,* vol. 47, 1 October 1971, p. 81.

[4] Richard Nixon, 'U.S. Foreign Policy for the 1970s' February 1971, p. 29.

[5] R. Cooper, 'The US and the Enlarged European Community' *The Round Table,* no. 244, October 1971, p. 576.

[6] *International Herald Tribune,* 15/16 December 1973.

[7] Edward Heath, *Old World, New Horizons,* Oxford University Press, London 1970.

[8] Ibid., p. 55.

[9] Leonard Beaton, 'The Strategic Issues' in Douglas Evans (ed.), *Destiny or Delusion,* Gollancz, London 1971, p. 176.

[10] W. Hallstein, quoted by R. Pryce in *The Political Future of the European Community,* John Marshbank, London 1962, p. 20.

[11] D. Mitrany, 'The Functional Approach to World Organisation' *International Affairs,* July 1948, pp. 351—60.

[12] D. Owen, *The Politics of Defence,* Cape, London 1972, p. 195.

[13] Lord Balniel, 'European Defence and European Security, *Survival* vol. XIII, no. 5, May 1971, p. 169.

[14] Michael Debré, 'The Principles of our Defence Policy', reprinted in *Survival,* vol. XII, no. 11, November 1970, p. 378.

[15] See Chapter 7, p. 123—4.

[16] Hedley Bull, 'Europe and the Wider World' *The Round Table,* no. 244, October 1971, p. 455.

[17] See Chapter 4, p. 62.

[18] One commentator on this chapter queried the adjective 'residual' as applied to the Soviet threat. By using it I do not mean to imply that the Soviet threat has diminished to the point where it can be regarded as negligible. Indeed, in terms of offensive capability the Soviets are probably more powerful than they have ever been. But in terms of the way in which we interpret their political intentions there is general agreement that they are much less hostile towards Europe than they were in the 1950s. For a more comprehensive analysis of the problem of threat assessment, the reader is referred to an article by the author, 'An Analysis of Threats', *International Relations,* October 1971.

[19] Richard Nixon, 'U.S. Foreign Policy for the 1970s', a report to the Congress, 18 February 1970, p. 20.

[20] T. Stanley, 'A Strategic Doctrine for NATO in the 1970s; *Orbis,* vol. XIII, no. 1, Spring 1969, p. 95.

[21] *Financial Times,* 30 July 1970, quoting M. Debré. (In the figures an exchange rate of £1·00 = F13·5 is used.)

[22] D. Lewardowski, 'National Defence Budget 1972', *Revue de Défense Nationale,* January 1972, p. 26.

[23] I. Smart, *Future Conditional: The Prospects for Anglo—French Nuclear Cooperation,* Adelphi Paper no. 78, International Institute for Strategic Studies, London 1971, p. 20.

[24] Ibid.

[25] R. Foch, *Europe and Technology,* Paris, Atlantic Institute, 1970, p. 48.

[26] A. Buchan, 'The Implications of a European System for Defence Technology', in *Defence, Technology and the Western Alliance,* Institute for Strategic Studies, London 1967, p. 19.

[27] F. Duchêne, 'A New European Defence Community', (ref 3), p. 80.

[28] H. Green, 'Prospects for European Arms Cooperation' in *The Defence of Western Europe,* ed. J.C. Garnett, Macmillan, London 1974, pp. 97–103.

[29] Ibid., p. 103.

7 The Enlarged Community and the European Security Conference

Crispin TICKELL

The views expressed here are those of the author and are not to be regarded as reflecting in any way the opinions or policies of the Foreign and Commonwealth office or of the British Government.

My subject is the enlarged European Community and the Conference on Security and Cooperation in Europe. There is an obvious connexion between the two. But my main theme will be less the connexion of the enlarged Community with the Conference than that of its nine member governments working together in the machinery of political cooperation. It has been these governments, sometimes in association with the Commission representing the Community, who have brought a distinctive and distinct contribution to the work of the Conference.

It is worth asking why the member governments of the Community should have chosen — as they did — to use the coordination of their policies towards the Conference as the first major test of their ability to work together. It could after all have been something else. But the idea of the Conference presented a particular challenge, and from the time when it became evident that the Conference was likely to happen, the Six, soon enlarged to Ten (and then regrettably reduced to Nine), began to prepare in earnest for it. What then were the main reasons?

First, although the idea of the Conference has an old and somewhat chequered history, the circumstances in which the Conference seemed likely to take place promised something new in European affairs. Policies were unformed, and those concerned in each capital had scarcely begun to think through the implications. Vested interests, whether national or international, had not yet crystallised. One thing only was certain: the Conference, if it took place, could not but affect the interests of Western as well as Eastern Europe, and needed therefore to be taken seriously.

Second, there was a more general feeling, perhaps I should describe it as a mood, that for the first time since the end of the war the political geography was changing, and that the Conference was bound to have some part to play, if only a small one, in a process which could lead to a new equilibrium in Europe. The prospect of an arrangement between East and West over the status of Germany and Berlin showed that one of the most dangerous of postwar problems might at last be defused. The apparent tendency towards isolationism in the USA meant that many Europeans were glad of the opportunity the Conference offered of bringing the North Americans as honorary Europeans into something with obvious significance for European security. Furthermore there was emerging a growing atmosphere of détente in which old antagonisms looked extensively out of date. Finally there was the enlargement of the Community itself. The Six had become the Nine. The Nine had established special relations with eleven more in Europe. Why then, and where, should the process stop? Those with any sense of history remembered the close links which the countries of Western Europe had enjoyed with those of Eastern Europe before the war, and hoped in a general rather than specific way that Europe might come together again.

Third, if for whatever reason there was to be a shift in the European equilibrium, the members of the Community and of course the Community itself had a very substantial interest in sharing their thoughts and if possible coordinating their policies. The Conference was one likely jousting ground. Preparation for it was anyway necessary. Why not do it together?

Few people then believed that the Nine, preoccupied by many other problems, including those flowing from enlargement, would be able to speak with one voice. The more optimistic hoped they might sing as a choir: that is to say choose the same song, practise it together, test the acoustics, and make sure that it had the right effect. That is what the Nine have tried to do, and so far — with one or two individual descants and usually but not always in the right key — have succeeded in doing.

The Conference has a long history, at least as an idea which Mr Molotov was talking about as early as 1954. In its present form the idea dates from 1966. Since then it has been a recurrent feature of Soviet and Warsaw Pact foreign policy statements. There was a hiccup in 1968 following the Russian invasion of Czechoslovakia. Perhaps somebody thought that a Conference dealing among other things with the inviolability of frontiers might not be appropriate in the circumstances. But by the following year the campaign for a Conference was resumed and has continued ever since.

It is worth remarking that when the campaign first started, and indeed since, the proposal was for 'a European Security Conference' or a 'pan-European Security Conference'. It is not for me to speculate on the

116

motives of those who proposed it, but one or two things seemed to stand out: first, that participation should be limited to Europeans (in other words the Americans and Canadians would be excluded); second, that it should have some of the aspects of a peace conference to consecrate the *status quo* in Europe — in other words the postwar frontiers marking the line of division between East and West. Third, a negative but important point, it should not deal with security in the sense in which we use the term, but rather establish new paper links between the European countries concerned (links which, like Christmas decorations, might be designed to make things look better than they really were).

It is not necessary to claim that the Western countries were not attracted by this prospectus for a Conference, although they did not reject the idea of a Conference itself. Between 1969 and 1972 they worked not only to change the character of any Conference but also to re-word the fine print of the prospectus on which the Conference could take place.

First, it was made clear that security in Europe could not be conceived of without the Americans and Canadians. Since the end of the war most of us have been aware of the vulnerability of Europe as a rich peninsula at the end of Asia. The new world had to be brought in to keep the balance of the old. North American participation was thus an essential condition for the holding of a Conference. It was eventually accepted.

Second, the notion that the Conference should be a sort of latter-day Congress of Vienna to endorse postwar frontiers in Central Europe was turned on its head. The Western countries insisted that only those directly concerned with the key problem of Germany were qualified to reach a satisfactory settlement. Thus until the Eastern Treaties and the Berlin Protocol had been concluded there could be no Conference.

Finally, the Western countries approached the problem of security in their own precise military way by putting forward separate proposals for mutual and balanced force reductions on the ground in the area of confrontation between the two military alliances. This did not imply that they believed the problems of security should be wholly removed from the scope of the Conference. They thought it most important that some military elements should remain, thus putting to the test protestations of good intentions and drawing attention to the central military problem of security. But it did mean that the most serious military problems could be dealt with properly between the parties directly involved.

A change of emphasis now followed. The prospects for promoting better cooperation among participants at the Conference now seemed better than those for their greater security. Cooperation between East and West in the widest sense of the term seemed anyway the principal requirement of the 1970s; indeed it was only in this way that the calls for détente which were heard on all sides could find practical expression. Eventually it was agreed that the correct title of the conference should be the Conference on Security and Cooperation in Europe. This in itself is not without significance. I am not sure this is what the original advocates of the conference really wanted.

The preparations for a conference of such scope involved many more on the Western side than the members of the Community either in its original or enlarged form. Given its underlying security aspect (particularly in the early days of preparation), the right place for coordination of Western policy as a whole towards the Conference was clearly the North Atlantic Alliance; and it was within the machinery of the Alliance that the essential policies and supporting proposals were slowly worked out. It is in some ways surprising that it should have been within a military alliance that proposals for — in the words of General de Gaulle's slogan — détente, entente and cooperation with the East should have been prepared. But this illustrates in vivid fashion not only the flexibility of the Alliance but the determination of its members to exploit changing circumstances in the world and to pursue cooperation with the East.

The Conference is not of course a bloc-to-bloc affair. It is a conference of states. This is a point to which all have attached importance from the beginning. The neutral and non-aligned countries have rightly wished to make their contribution. The last thing anyone wanted was for the two military alliances to perform as such at the Conference, with perhaps the neutral and non-aligned countries acting as a sort of bloc of their own, tipping their weight first one way and then the other. The Western countries have made a particular effort to work with the neutral and non-aligned countries, and to take full account of their ideas on how to lower the barriers to cooperation in Europe. In the event these countries have very much come out into the sun. It has been good to see them exerting the sort of influence which some of them did in the past.

But how were the Nine involved in this process? By the time the new machinery for political consultation had been set up, a lot of the ground work of preparation for the Conference within the Alliance had already been done. Moreover the Six, as they then were, recognised that the security aspects were properly a matter for the Alliance and not for them.

In the field of cooperation, however, it was obvious that there remained an immense amount of work in which the members of the Community had a special interest. It was equally obvious that a big gap remained between the definition of long term objectives and the determination of the tactical means and appropriate procedures for the attainment of these objectives on which so much — unfortunately — depended. In mid-1971 the work began and has continued with increasing intensity ever since.

It is not possible in this chapter to analyse in detail the particular problems with which the Nine have dealt. Some were of long term importance for the future of cooperation among the Nine as well as for the Conference itself; some — just as difficult at the time — were ephemeral. But they formed part of a general approach towards the Conference which might broadly be described as follows: first, to secure the widest possible acceptance of an approach to détente based on practical improvements in specific areas; and second, to encourage the lowering of barriers within Europe by developing cooperation in its various aspects, and particularly by promoting freer movement of people, ideas and information. We also have more defensive aims: to maintain Western unity in general and the movement towards West European integration in particular; and to maintain a realistic atmosphere, free from illusions, in which people could clearly see the prospects before them without undue optimism or equally undue pessimism.

Together we were able to work out detailed and practical ideas which were put to the East during the long months of bargaining at the preparatory talks at Helsinki from November 1972 to June 1973. Our purpose was, in the words of the NATO Communiqué of May 1972, to determine whether enough 'common ground existed among the participants to warrant reasonable expectations that a Conference would produce satisfactory results'.

The work of the Nine fell into two broad categories: first on the economic and technical aspects of cooperation; and second, on the political, humanitarian and cultural aspects.

Although the Conference was a conference of states, it was obvious from the start that the European Community as such would have a large interest in economic and technical cooperation. The questions for the member governments, working together in the new machinery of political cooperation, were first how the Commission should be brought into their deliberations, and second how it should make its voice heard (in accordance with the relevant provisions of the Treaty of Rome) on matters where the competence of the Community was involved. These problems are easier to state than to solve. Major issues of policy are hidden behind what look like problems of procedure.

The first problem was tackled by the establishment of an *ad hoc* group consisting of representatives from ministries of foreign affairs of the member states of the Community and from the Commission. This group was made responsible to the political directors (or deputy undersecretaries at ministries of foreign affairs) again with a representative of the Commission. They in turn were made responsible to the foreign ministers with the President of the Commission (or his representative). So far so good. But how should the work already done in the Alliance be coordinated? How should the machinery of the Commission be set to work? How should the Nine balance their different obligations and maintain clear government control? All that may be stated here is that these problems were eventually solved.

The second problem was still more difficult. On the one hand the Commission had the right to represent the Community in international organisations when Community competence was involved. On the other the Conference was one of states, and the representation of even one international organisation could greatly have complicated things. We did not want to precipitate a situation in which organisations different in kind from the Community would demand equal status and the same treatment. In the end, after long debate, not made easier by doubts over the definition of Community competence, it was agreed that representatives of the Commission should form part of the national delegation of the country exercising the Presidency of the Community, but should speak as members of the Commission when questions of Community competence arose. It has yet to be seen how well this compromise will work in practice, considering the obvious difficulties.

Concerning the scope of the Conference, the idea of improved economic and technical cooperation appears reasonable and everyone would wish to subscribe to it. But the question of how to set about it at a conference of 35 states of varying economic systems and specific obligations to others is extremely difficult.

Thus the Conference would not be the right place for an arrangement which pertained only to, say, the members of the Community on the one hand and certain East European states on the other. The Conference cannot be a trade conference, and no trade negotiations as such will take place under the auspices, but we hope that it will give an impetus which will lead to specific trade or other forms of economic negotiation later. It is for this reason that the Community, represented by the Commission, cannot but take a close interest in certain aspects of the Conference's work, in particular that on future commercial exchanges.

The arrangements made among the member governments for dealing with the political, humanitarian and cultural aspects of the Conference are more easily described. A special sub-committee — at the same level as the *ad hoc* group but without of course the Commission — was set up to prepare for the Conference. This sub-committee was made responsible to the political directors, and the political directors in turn to their foreign ministers.

The problems here have been like those of any foreign office writ large. Different interests and preoccupations have had to be reconciled. For example the Germans have always seen the Conference as an aspect of their Ostpolitik. The French and the Italians have naturally been concerned by the Mediterranean aspect, and the Danes by the Nordic one. Others have been concerned lest work among the Nine should cut across work in the Alliance or threaten its cohesion. However, I think this danger has in fact been averted and that effective working arrangements have been established. The Nine, moreover, have had to reckon with their bilateral relationships with third parties including the USA and the Soviet Union.

Not surprisingly the various groups have had to meet frequently. Usually they have met, at different levels, in the capital of the country holding the Presidency of the Community. But in the circumstances of the Conference meetings have also taken place at Helsinki and now in Geneva. I cannot pretend that I have been to every meeting of the CSCE sub-committee and *ad hoc* group, or of the political directors or of the foreign ministers, but I think I have been to most of them since the beginning of 1972. They have been an interesting and rewarding experience.

Not everything has worked well all the time. It may be worth describing what I see as the weaknesses of the system, if only because it helps to bring out its underlying strength and flexibility. The lack of a secretariat has meant that each country occupying the Presidency has had to wrestle with the task of preparing agendas, codifying papers, dealing with proposals and amendments, and of course producing compromises. Information about meetings has sometimes arrived too late to permit proper preparation. Conflicting papers are often circulated at a meeting and it is unclear which if any of them is the basis of discussion. I have on occasion witnessed participants commenting at length on the wrong paper. Worse still I have done so myself.

An additional problem is the language in which the committee discussion takes place. I should judge that two-thirds of the time we speak French and one-third of the time we speak English. Most participants are therefore working most of the time in a foreign language and the finer points can sometimes be lost. Criticism can sound harsher than intended and political points go unregistered.

At the next level up, and taking a worm's eye view, political directors, themselves very busy men with correspondingly wide responsibilities, sometimes arrive at meetings relatively unbriefed and with bright ideas which have already been considered, accepted or rejected further down. Thus old issues get reopened, and those concerned with higher matters of policy get entangled — sometimes I fear with relish — in the snares of drafting or redrafting. Sometimes there is conflict between decisions reached in some cosy capital and the ability of those in a smoke-filled negotiating room far away to put them into effect. Things have often moved too fast for the process of consultation up the hierarchy.

There have also been times when moving at the pace of the slowest has led to gnashing of teeth; others when one of the Nine has, perhaps due to a misunderstanding, moved ahead of his colleagues and spoken out too boldly in public or appeared to abandon a common position. Few of us have not done this at one time or another. Such slips are inevitable and thus forgivable, but obviously they should not take place.

What have been the achievements of these protracted efforts? Most important we have in fact succeeded in working out common policies and putting them into effect. From the beginning of the preparatory consultations in Helsinki we found that the very effectiveness of the Nine, above all in the day-to-day business of the consultations, had given us unexpected responsibilities of leadership. For reasons of their own (not perhaps unconnected with the evolution of their bilateral relations with the Soviet Union) the Americans preferred to play a relatively modest role. And so while coordination among the fifteen members of the Alliance has remained good, it has been increasingly the Nine who not only provided the motor but sat at the steering wheel (which they found was usually, but not always, attached to the front wheels).

The Nine, and behind them the Fifteen, soon showed that they were much better prepared for the Helsinki consultations than anyone else. They sometimes had their difficulties, but at least they were rarely surprised. For all the occasional incoherence of the discussions among the Nine — or perhaps because of it — we had over the months thought of just about every idea, possibility or manoeuvre which might occur. By thrashing out among ourselves French ideas about cultural exchanges, German ideas about economic cooperation, Danish ideas about freer movement of people, British ideas about military measures to build confidence — the list is not endless but it is long — we had already identified most of the questions which later arose from different vantage points, and had taken decisions among ourselves in the light of them.

Each member of the Nine developed its own speciality, and spoke in support of it on the basis of a common position. This had obvious tactical value as it gave the West as a whole a measure of negotiating flexibility.

Finally we found that the Nine could sometimes deal more easily with the other participants at the Conference than the fifteen members of the Alliance. I believe that the neutral and non-aligned countries found it more congenial to work with a group which had no military background than with either of the two military alliances. On the Western side the organisation of work and coordination between the Nine and the Fifteen remained effective. If the smaller wheel revolved more quickly, its cogs meshed without difficulty with the larger and slower wheel of the Alliance.

How did this machinery of consultation and coordination affect the proceedings in Helsinki? The best answer is to be found in the Final Recommendations which emerged from the consultations at Helsinki between November 1972 and June 1973. The language may not always be as elegant as we would have wished but the substance wholly reflects the Western idea of what the Conference should be about; in short, a conference to deal with detailed and specific problems falling into three main groups, rather than a declaratory affair of peace, brotherhood and high principle. As the British Foreign Secretary said at the first stage of the Conference at Helsinki:

> The people of our countries will not thank or congratulate us for adding more solemn declarations to the world's archives different from other such documents — only in the signatures upon them.

A balance was in fact struck at Helsinki which gave those three main groups — politico—military, economic and human — equal importance and linked them together. It is of fundamental importance to us that this balance should be maintained. Above all we want measures which will advance cooperation not merely between the participating governments but between the people of the participating states. The Final Recommendations fully reflect this sentiment, and we shall hold the other participants to what they have so clearly undertaken to do. At both the first ministerial stage, and the second more detailed committee stage, the Nine have worked as well together as during the preliminary consultations. It has not been easy. The mere size of delegations with their teeming experts created a measure of incoherence and uncertainty at the beginning of the work in Geneva. But within a few weeks the habits of Helsinki had triumphed, and the members of the Nine at their various levels were once more pulling in harness.

It is too early for self-congratulation. Things could easily go wrong. This time others are just as well prepared as we are. Differences of emphasis between the Nine could assume greater importance. It would be a mistake to pretend that they are united in everything. But I think all would agree that the common interest is in the last resort greater than the sum of our individual interests and that the governments of the Nine will continue to fashion their policies on this assumption.

It is also too early to judge what effects this enterprise in cooperation may have in other fields. In the last few months we have seen other examples of cooperation among the Nine. Cooperation seems to grow in response to the requirements made of it. There is an indefinable feeling that the whole process is both quickening and deepening. If so those of us who undertook the pilot project for the CSCE will perhaps look back with pride on their success and the precedent that they set for others.

8   Desirability, Objectives and Possibilities of a Common Ostpolitik

Pierre HASSNER

In a book devoted to the question: 'Can the European Community have an Ostpolitik?' the task of writing about the desirability, the objectives, and the possibilities of this Ostpolitik is both easy and impossible. Easy because, since the topic broadly coincides with that of the whole study, the author should be able to draw on the contributions of his colleagues; impossible because, whether on the difficulties of making separate foreign policies merge into a common one, or on its economic, military or diplomatic content, he finds next to nothing to add to the contributions of Frans Alting von Geusau, John Pinder, John Garnett and Crispin Tickell.

In order to find a possible space for a useful complement to these excellent analyses, I shall, then, concern myself primarily with the broadly political dimension as opposed to the specific and the substantive, and more with its Eastern than with its Western aspect. In other terms, I shall ask myself: 'How should or could a common Ostpolitik, if it existed, influence the East?' rather than: 'What are the degree and forms of West European unity which would make such an Ostpolitik possible and desirable?'

However, the two sides are obviously linked, and probably more so every day, just as the definition of the objectives of a common Ostpolitik depends upon one's view both of the desirable and of the possible. One of the most striking aspects of East—West relations is the mirror image quality, whether symmetrical or contrasting, of our usual assumptions about them, in spite of the very complex combinations of structural analogies and differences between Western and Eastern Europe, between EEC and Comecon, or between NATO and WTO. The question of whom one should address — whether individual East European countries, Eastern Europe as a whole minus the Soviet Union, or the whole Eastern camp — is neither identical with nor independent from the question of who should conduct the policy — the Community, its member states, or the West as a whole?

In turn, the questions of who and towards whom cannot be divorced from the basic one: 'What is one trying to achieve — greater independence from Eastern Europe, greater domestic freedom for its citizens, or greater links with Western Europe?

Finally, the question arises whether, given the structural realities and the present trends in each half of Europe, the problem of an Ostpolitik is most accurately formulated in terms of objectives and strategies or, rather, in terms of the indirect, and partly unpredictable and unmanageable consequences of social and historical processes. The lack of unity and of priority for an Ostpolitik in the West, the tightening of the centralised control from the top and the vigilant opposition to external influences in the East, have made the limitations of Western policies towards Eastern Europe obvious to all. On the other hand, the pressures of economic and technological interdependence are no less obvious, particularly to communist governments incapable of living in autarky but unwilling to open up their societies. Western societies, however, are even more vulnerable to the pressures and the constraints, the appeals and the strains of interdependence. The real problem, then, may be less that of the deliberate policies directed by Western and Eastern Europe towards each other than that of their respective responses to common challenges or to their respective crises, and of the consequences which these responses have on their mutual relations. What, for instance, is the impact of the current energy crisis and, more generally, of the economic situation of Western Europe on its economic relations with the East? On the other hand, the new social and political instability in Western Europe has several aspects which, potentially at least, affect East—West relations: the possibility of left wing coalitions reaching power in Italy or in France, the actual change of régime in Portugal and in Greece, the uncertainties linked to the succession problem in Spain and in Yugoslavia — all this goes beyond the domestic politics of West European States and the evolution of regions like the Mediterranean and the Balkans which cut across the division between Western and Eastern Europe. At a time when the nations of the European Community are more preoccupied with their internal problems, with their relations with the USA or with the oil producers than with formulating an Ostpolitik, it brings the East—West dimension within these problems themselves.

From individual national interests to a common Ostpolitik?

Perhaps before exploring these complexities and ambiguities, a few initial definitions and questions will be useful. To understand what a common

126

Ostpolitik might mean, it is perhaps best to distinguish between the types of interests and situations of specific countries of Western Europe as a whole, and of the Community as such.

Arnold Wolfers has suggested a distinction between 'possession goals', i.e. specific and direct ones, and 'milieu goals', or general and indirect ones. This seems to apply particularly well to the interests of various West European countries towards East European ones or towards Eastern Europe in general. Some countries, through their geographical situation or historical traditions, have specific interests, which tie them to East European countries through specific conflicts or ties. This is, for instance, the case of Austria with Hungary, Czechoslovakia and Yugoslavia, Italy with Yugoslavia, the Scandinavian countries via Finland, or with Poland or Russia (as in the present disputes about oil). Other countries have no such specific problems or ties. For them relations with Eastern Europe are just one case for applying a general attitude — for instance in favour of peace, détente, trade and cooperation. This is the case of Belgium or the Netherlands and to a great extent, of Britain. In between this general attitude and specific possession goals are Wolfers's 'milieu goals', having to do with a country's interest in the structure of the regional balance or a system and in its own situation within it. For most West European countries Ostpolitik is less than a direct, specific interest in some territorial or population issue, and more than a general commitment to trade or peace; it has to do with an attitude towards Europe's perennial problem, that of the actual or potential, joint or conflicting, power of the Soviet Union and of Germany, with how to solve the dilemma of Germany being either too strong or too weak for the continent, or with how to contain the Soviet Union while keeping Germany within a collective framework.

This has been, in particular, a traditional French concern, to which both the policy of the Fourth Republic (centred on West European integration) and that of the Fifth (centred, under de Gaulle, upon a pan-European concert of states) tried to bring an answer.

In recent times West European politics have been more centred upon the intra West European Paris—London—Bonn triangle, with the successive stresses on the Franco—British and Franco—German relationship. The question, then, is whether, concerning Ostpolitik, different traditions and interests are more likely to lead to conflicts than to a common policy.

It is true that the three countries exemplify the three typical situations: the Federal Republic is the only one who has massive direct interests in Eastern Europe — through her relations with her neighbours, and particularly with the GDR. Every possible link, positive or negative,

127

through borders and people, economic incentives and military security, makes West Germany crucial for Eastern Europe and vice versa. One of the main problems of a community Ostpolitik has always been whether it would have to embrace the specific interests of one of its main participants — Germany. France represents the paradox of having no direct problems, no major interests in the East, yet having been a path breaker and a very active participant in the détente game. The reason, of course, is that, especially under de Gaulle, in the transition periods of 1944–1946 and 1963–1968, she had a strong interest in the reshaping of the European system, in Europe's role between the superpowers, or in France's own role between Germany and Russia. As for Britain, with the limited exception of Harold Macmillan's attempts at playing the 'honest broker' between the USA and the Soviet Union in 1959/60, she has shown little active interest except in the most general terms.

It would be wrong, however, to draw the conclusion that these differing traditional interests are an insuperable obstacle to the emergence of a common Ostpolitik. Rather, it is striking how little of a bone of contention relations with the East have been in West European politics, except in de Gaulle's time. Even then, what seemed worrying and unacceptable to France's Western partners was much less the Eastern dimension of the 'Europe from the Atlantic to the Urals' policy than the accompanying downgrading of Atlantic and West European links. Of course the specific character of Germany's situations and interests has always created a problem because Germany was either more reluctant or more eager towards détente than her partners. But after both de Gaulle's enterprise and, more importantly, Willy Brandt's have spent their course, we have witnessed, rather a certain convergence in the respective Ostpolitik of the three members of the triangle. Neither of them is against détente, neither is under any illusion, at least in the short run, that it will bring reunification for Germany or a central balancing role for France. Differences in ultimate goals and in style remain, and they are often paradoxical: Germany, who has possession goals or bilateral interests, has tended, after the completion of its treaties with its Eastern neighbours, to emphasise the multilateralisation of détente and of Ostpolitik, just as, within the EEC, it had always favoured supranational institutions. France, on the other hand, whose goals are 'milieu' ones and whose interest is either the maintenance of the old multilateral system or the setting up of a new one, in order to compensate Germany's superior weight, has, under de Gaulle and Pompidou, favoured an independent policy based on bilateral relations with various partners. Even though it was in the forefront of détente, it has been lukewarm, at best, towards its institutionalisation on the pan-European level, particularly in the military field. Britain under Edward Heath has shown a similar reticence based on different motives.

Today, however, these differences which have never been really dramatic tend to wither away. France and Germany each tend to get closer to their logical respective positions, the former with Giscard d'Estaing, rediscovering the virtues of common institutions and the latter, with Helmut Schmidt, giving precedence to multiple bilateralism. Britain seems more forthcoming in the two East–West multilateral negotiations. All in all, it is not too optimistic to observe a real convergence in the Ostpolitiks of the major West European states. This has gone far enough to permit a real coordination, including an agreement on a common strategy at the CSCE and on the role of the Community in the Conference.

It has not gone far enough, however, to enable one to speak of a broader common policy, and even less of an agreement to transform it into a common policy of the Community and to entrust the Brussels Commission with its formulation or its implementation.

Even in economic relations with the East, while bilateral treaties have been denounced and communist countries have to negotiate with the Commission after 1 January 1975, the individual countries of the Nine have preserved their freedom of action for industrial cooperation. While they have shown – in particular at the CSCE – a remarkable interest in preserving the legitimacy and the possible role of the Community as such, its interests remain distinct from those of Western Europe as a whole, let alone those of the various member states themselves.

But what, indeed, are these interests which would constitute the goals of an Ostpolitik for the Community? Do they consist, above all, in the safeguarding of its identity and of its autonomy? This is how it often looks from the outside. Does this concern for identity and autonomy lead to a concern for recognition? This raises the question of how much this recognition is worth, and, more specifically, whether being recognised and dealt with officially by the East is worth extension of the same recognition to COMECON, thereby abandoning, to a certain extent at least, the Community's claim to originality. And this, in turn, leads to the basic dilemma of any Ostpolitik, a dilemma made more acute, in the case of the Community, by its own inchoate and uncertain status: should it be interested essentially in protecting its own development or in modifying its environment? The former priority amounts to a primacy of the defensive, hence in avoiding Eastern interference in West European unification. The latter means a primacy of the offensive, i.e. the acceptance of some risks of Eastern interference in or indirect influence upon West European unification in order to exert some influence on East European affairs. This dilemma has sprung up again and again, particularly at the CSCE in connection with pan-European institutions. But to give an answer at all one would have to specify what influence one is seeking on whose and on which affairs. Which brings up to our true subject — the objectives of a common Ostpolitik and the extent to which realities in Eastern Europe make them desirable and realistic.

Dilemmas, priorities, constraints: permanent realities and specific problems

Ever since Stalin's death and the first 'thaw' of 1953, the Western powers, taken collectively, regionally or individually have faced a number of common questions in their relations with Eastern Europe. But the answers to these questions vary with the evolution of the East and with the identity of the Western partner.

The first two dilemmas have to do with the question who in its simplest form, namely: 'What countries or organisation should the policy be aimed at?'

The first one is: 'Should one treat East Germany like any other state?' Until quite recently, but especially in the phase of dynamic and selective détente, between 1963 and 1968, when competing strategies were trying to advance various forms and combinations of German and European reunification, they all, with the partial exception of Egon Bahr's 'little steps' and 'change through *rapprochement*' policy drew a distinction between the normal communist states, which were seen as corresponding more or less to some national reality, and the GDR, an artificial creation that would become isolated in the process of détente and would be condemned to extinction by a European settlement. In spite of some partial successes with the East Europeans, this policy was seen to have failed by 1967 and was buried for good by the treaty between the two German states, their admission to the UN, and the almost universal recognition of the GDR which followed in 1972–73.

But the problem has not been buried with the policy, and, interestingly enough, it is particularly seen to remain open at the level of the EEC. The two German 'enemy brothers' have, as could be expected, both the most tense or antagonistic relationship and the closest ties of any East–West pair of countries. The best example of this is the intra-German trade which was considered as domestic (hence not submitted to Common

130

Market tariffs) both at the time of greatest mutual hostility and non-recognition and today, when both Germanies are considered as sovereign states and when the GDR insists on refusing the concept of a common nationhood and of any special ties which might get in the way of *Abgrenzung* policy. Obviously there is a tacit bargain there, between the Federal Republic's desire to keep as many links as possible with the GDR and as many symbols of the possibility, one day, of some institutional re-association, and the GDR's own economic advantage. But this does raise a problem for their respective Western and Eastern partners, and especially for the former. For a long time the issue of German reunification has played a role in the debate about European integration. A European solution was seen as the only way of making German reunification acceptable to the other Europeans or her division acceptable to the Germans themselves. Today both the federalist ideal of the United States of Europe and the national ideal of German reunification seem to have lost most of their credibility for the foreseeable future. Under present conditions of West Germany by itself, being by far the strongest and healthiest member of the Community, certainly the prevalent feeling among the other eight would be to welcome her division. Yet both their general interest in communication with Eastern Europe and, even more, avoiding a conflict with the FRG lead them to support the latter's special ties with the GDR even at some economic and logical cost regarding Common Market regulations. Today, this is not a very burning and worrying issue. If, however, evolution in either Germany or in both were to raise the possibility of a significant change in the nature of their relations, the German problem would come back where it used to be, i.e. at the centre both of European integration and of Ostpolitik. And it will be as desirable as ever not to let the two dimensions conflict but to make of the former the preferred framework for the latter.

The second dilemma, too, has both an historical aspect, which is no longer relevant, and a permanent one which may reassure itself in the long run. The question is: 'Should priority be given to the states of Eastern Europe or to the Soviet Union?' More than for the first dilemma, it has always been obvious that there was no exclusive answer. To give a straight priority to the Kremlin would mean to help it consolidate its empire and make it yet more rigid and exclusive. On the other hand, to try to encourage divisions in the empire and detach its weakest links means not only alienating the Soviet Union (which no Western power is interested in doing, if only for strategic and economic reasons), but risking counter-reactions on her part which would tighten the very domination over Eastern Europe one was trying to ease.

Obviously the trend in Western Ostpolitiks has gone from avoiding the first danger to avoiding the second. The great dividing line is, of course, represented by the invasion of Czechoslovakia, through which the Soviet Union very effectively made the point that she was to be the main interlocutor and pacesetter of East–West détente. West Germany may, as a consequence, have moved from a perhaps imprudent preference for the states of Eastern Europe in spite of Moscow's opposition, under Foreign Minister Schröder, and to a lesser extent, during the first years of the Great Coalition, to a slightly excessive precedence given to Moscow after the events of Prague. In American policy, 'peaceful engagement' was meant first as a way of detaching the satellites from the Soviet Union, then as a more multilateral concept which for a time excluded East Germany but finally included all communist states, with a clear priority to the bilateral détente with the Soviet Union (balanced by bilateral relationships with East European countries like Rumania).

France, under de Gaulle, had engaged in a more methodical attempt at balancing between the Soviet Union and her smaller allies. 'Europe from the Atlantic to the Urals' occasionally seemed to signify a Franco–Soviet agreement that would replace Soviet–American hegemony; on other occasions it signified a revolt of small and middle European nations, both East and West, against both hegemonies. But after 1968, the balance clearly tilted in favour of the Soviet Union, even though, in particular at the CSCE, France has tried to continue to combine the desire to be second to none in friendship with the Soviet Union, and a sympathetic stand towards the desire of small countries like Rumania to play an independent role and to maintain bilateral relations with Western states.

For an Ostpolitik of Western Europe, and even more of the EEC, as such, the problem is even more difficult than for individual countries. For the USA, the priority of the dialogue between the two superpowers is obvious even though it does not preclude them from using bilateral relations with each other's allies in order to improve their own bargaining position. For West Germany, obviously the priority goes to relations with the GDR and with the Soviet Union, as the main influence over the latter, even though Eastern Europe plays a role within an indirect strategy of 'multilateralising Ostpolitik'. For France, as for the other West European countries, there is a tendency to prefer the Soviet Union as a bilateral interlocutor, for prestige, for political and more recently for economic reasons, but there is also an awareness of having more in common with the smaller East European countries and of having an interest in helping them to increase their freedom of action which in most cases leads to a greater opening to communication with Western Europe.

But for Western Europe as such and, even more, for the EEC itself the problem is much more complicated. A logical and almost aesthetic search for greater symmetry favours finding a counterpart in some kind of an organised Eastern Europe, with which to open a dialogue. The trouble is that such an Eastern European union or organisation does not exist. Even if it existed, formal symmetry would not prevent it from being no match for Western Europe. One runs here into the familiar dilemma that a purely continental balance is impossible in Europe because Eastern Europe without Russia is too weak in face of Western Europe and, with Russia, it is too strong. However that may be, it is clear that, for the time being, any attempt at organising, much less institutionalising the cooperation between East European states without the Soviet Union is barred by the latter, who maintains a preponderant power in the Warsaw Treaty Organisation and in Comecon, even though it may sometimes rule by negotiation rather than by a simple *fiat*.

The Community is, then, faced with the dilemma of dealing with a Comecon dominated by the Soviet Union or with individual East European countries. In the first case, she runs into a double ambiguity. She may by tacitly or officially recognising Comecon help ensure her own recognition by the East, but also weaken her claim to originality and her sense of identity by accepting a false symmetry with an organisation dominated by the Soviet Union and based on principles having nothing to do with supranational integration among equals; she may, also, help institutionalise the links of East European countries with the West, but at the cost of reinforcing their subordination towards the Soviet Union. Some of these countries themselves, like Hungary and Poland, seem to believe that multilateralisation, both within Comecon and between EEC and the latter ultimately helps their own independence. Others, like Rumania, fear that it threatens theirs or, like Yugoslavia, fear to be left out of the mainstream of East—West economic relations if these are channelled through existing sub-regional organisations.

The second road, then, that of bilateral relations with individual socialist countries, has its own share of ambiguities. Bilateral relations of the EEC as such expose it to the accusation of applying a neocolonialist policy of 'divide and rule' in order to convert smaller East European states into satellites. More importantly, they may either be blocked by the Soviet Union or weaken the Community's own claim for a common Ostpolitik as opposed to the separate economic policies of its member states.

Again, no clearcut answer is possible. The likely emergence of a pan-European framework out of the CSCE and under the Geneva

133

Economic Commission for Europe, may mitigate the dilemma by combining a general multilateral element, a role for sub-regional organisations (without their having to formally recognise each other), and a legitimate role for single states and bilateral relations. But the real answer depends on a political choice over the nature and future of European politics in general.

The key to the third dilemma, then, lies in the third and fourth, which have to do with these more general choices — for Eastern Europe and for the evolution of European and international relations in general.

To begin with, should one try to encourage primarily de-Stalinisation or de-satellisation, i.e. internal liberalisation or external independence? The distinction is well established today. In the long run both roads may very well converge as the example of Yugoslavia seems to show; the struggle for independence against the Soviet Union led to an opening to the West and, ultimately, to domestic liberalisation and conversely, today, domestic hardening seems to go hand in hand with a certain *rapprochement* towards the Soviet Union. But clearly, for the time being, Hungary, buying its internal reforms at the price of total orthodoxy in international affairs, and Rumania, where the primary concern for external independence has served to justify the permanence of the leader's cult or of forced industrialisation, indicate the two divergent roads possible today for East European states, short of total alignment on Moscow, Bulgarian style: Hungary's 'intra-bloc consumerism' and Rumania's 'intra-bloc nationalism'. The margin of action of both seems to have been steadily reduced in the years since 1968. By a mixture of patience, firmness, relative flexibility and occasional brutality, the Soviet Union has succeeded in re-establishing a considerable measure of cohesion within her sphere, which, in a troubled and chaotic world stands out as a rigid, uninspired but solid island of order if not of law.[1] But, if the East European countries themselves have so little space for diversity, the role of West European policies in influencing their choices and their evolution is obviously even more restricted. Yet inevitably, West Europeans have had and still have to express a preference, whether tacitly or explicitly, through their action or their inaction.

De Gaulle was obviously interested in encouraging aspirations to independence and disdainful of ideologies and internal régimes; hence his lack of interest or support for the Czechoslovak experience, in which he saw the work of intellectuals who were incompetent at the diplomatic levels. By contrast, Willy Brandt's Ostpolitik was obviously based on the same type of assumptions as the 'Hungarian model': rather than encouraging nationalism (which in East Germany's case might in fact lead to more self-closure and intransigence towards West Germany), his gamble was on encouraging the self-confidence both of Soviet and East German leaders in their respective rule and the prosperity of their societies, in the hope that ultimately stability would produce relaxation both within societies, in their relations with the West, and even in their relations with each other. As for the USA, while it has an obvious interest in the maintenance of Chinese and Yugoslav independence, and while its interest in Eastern Europe is very reduced anyway, the logic of its dialogue with the Soviet Union, of its concern for the stability of an interdependent world, and for the creation of common interests between East and West in order to achieve a 'stable structure of peace' points towards a preference for slow evolution within the Eastern bloc under the surveillance and within the limits of tolerance of the Soviet Union.

For Western Europe and the Community as such, the problems are somewhat similar to those we described within the framework of the preceding dilemma. In a situation where the Soviet Union has a conservative view of the authority structure within her empire and within the various communist states, and has the means to enforce this view, the scope for de-satellisation is very limited and for de-Stalinisation only slightly less so. The West Europeans are primarily interested in maintaining and developing contacts and communication, extending from business to culture, with the East.

Clearly, as shown in the cases of Hungary and Rumania, the incentives for this opening, on the Eastern side, can come both from the imperatives of domestic reform and from those of external autonomy towards the Soviet Union; but its structural foundations are better secured in the first case than in the second. While Rumania's desire for Western support to counterbalance dependence on the Soviet Union leads it into daringly exposed special relationships with Western organisations (from the EEC to the IMF) and into attracting Western capital as vigorously as possible, this collaboration runs into fairly severe difficulties due to the economic, social and political rigidities of the Rumanian system. Conversely, Hungary's domestic reforms (particularly concerning the price structure) enable her to be, in many respects, really integrated into the Western system of economic relationships, with the advantages and also the vulnerabilities (in particular to inflation) which go with it. Hungary's orthodox foreign policy enables it to be more relaxed concerning human and cultural relations with the West, being less exposed to the accusation of changing sides.

It seems clear that, to the extent that Western Europe's interest is in maintaining communication and spreading its own economic, social and cultural influence, this interest leads it to favour the Hungarian model. On the other hand, to the extent that, under the umbrella and within the constraints of the present bipolar structure, characterised by the balance and the concert of the two superpowers, Western Europe wants to preserve the preconditions for a future European reassertion, it has an interest in encouraging whatever national and regional autonomy is possible in Eastern Europe against Soviet hegemony.

This raises, then, the ultimate question which no longer concerns West Europeans' notions about Eastern Europe but about themselves, not about Ostpolitik but about politics as such. The dilemma is: 'Should one rely essentially on socio-economic trends or on diplomatic activity? On the independent action of states or the interdependent structure of societies? On a Gaullist or a Monnetist model?' The answer obviously depends upon the nature and role of the Europe one is trying to build. In its internal structure, should it be a Europe of the states or a federal union? In its external relations, should it be aimed at becoming a great power able to modify the world balance and to challenge the supremacy of the two superpowers, or at transforming the nature of international relations and at challenging the prevalence of power politics?

Various combinations of priorities and motives, and of national, regional, pan-European or global unity and diversity are possible according to the answer given to these fundamental dilemmas. It is clear that no simple answer is going to prevail. As far as the structure of Western Europe is concerned, de Gaulle's Europe of the States has proved its failure to unite on a common economic or foreign policy, yet a federal United States of Europe is clearly not in sight. What does seem both possible and desirable is an empirical and variable combination of common institutions (the Community, the European Parliament, the Council of Ministers) and of inter-governmental cooperation. Similarly, Western Europe is clearly not likely to have, in the foreseeable future, the degree of unity, the political will or, indeed, the desire to place a priority on making an all-out effort to become one of the world's five major independent centres of power; nor, conversely, can it entertain the hope of having made such a success of the Community method that it can transform the nature of relations with or within other areas, especially when they include other types of political régimes or of economic situations. But, here again, a much more modest version of these goals, pursued in combination, does make sense and does carry implications for relations with Eastern Europe.

The first priority, for Western Europe, and particularly for the Community as such is bound to be the protection of whatever degree of unity has been achieved through the Common Market and of the further construction of a European union. In this sense, there is a minimum meaning of a Community Ostpolitik which is essentially defensive, being aimed at safeguarding the original character of the Community from being diluted whether in pan-European economic cooperation or in a new security system which might mean a *de facto* neutralisation under the surveillance of the two superpowers, or of the most immediately and massively present of the two. This concern, entirely legitimate as such, has sometimes been pushed to such lengths that it has seemed to jeopardise the very possibility of a positive Ostpolitik. This may have been the case with the common agricultural policy or with external tariffs, where too little regard may have been granted to the consequences for East European economies, or with the position of the community representative in the second (economic) basket of the CSCE. Similarly, on the question of permanent pan-European institutions or of a 'follow-up' of the CSCE as well as on the question of the 'European clause' in MBFR, the entirely desirable priority of removing any potential obstacle from the path towards a European federal union or a common defence has sometimes seemed to be pursued with far more intensity than the positive progress towards these very goals.

This may come from a feeling that the precondition for pursuing the process of European integration is to safeguard it from hostile or dissolving influences and to maintain a certain capacity for independent action and reaction towards the outside world. In face of the military superiority of the Soviet Union and the USA, of the economic leverage of the USA and the oil producers, a certain amount of Gaullism, or preoccupation with independence and with the power of resistance may be necessary for protecting what is left of Monnetism, or of the attempt to build new types of structures and relationships.

This attempt at maintaining or acquiring a specific weight and avoiding being at the mercy of external objections, protection or control, inevitably has an impact on the positive, day-to-day side of Ostpolitik, i.e. the management of the Community's direct relations with, and indirect impact on, its Eastern neighbours. These relations and this impact are primarily economic. As such, beyond the obvious advantages of trade and investment they may acquire a special value in a time of crisis of search for alternative sources of raw materials and alternative markets. Unfortunately, from a purely economic point of view, it seems that the attraction of the Soviet Union has increased and that of smaller East European countries who run balance of payments deficits and have (with partial exceptions in the case of Poland and Rumania) no coal or oil to offer, has decreased.

It remains true, however, that to the extent that East—West economic relations are based on some kind of complementarity and of mutual affinity, these exist more between the USA and the Soviet Union than between Western and Eastern Europe. A certain division of labour, based both on dimensions and on traditions, tends to emerge. This is even more the case when, beyond strictly economic exchange and cooperation, one goes to social and cultural contacts and influences. There are several reasons which make it even more important for the Community than for the USA (if one excepts the special case of the Jewish community) not to separate economic relations from wider exchanges and communications involving ideas and individuals and, furthermore, to emphasise particularly, in this respect, contacts with Eastern Europe. These are the spiritual heritage upon which the Community has to build if a European identity is to make a distinctive mark in a world of generalised interdependence, historical and geographic proximity to Eastern Europe, human links through common national origins in the case of Germany and travel. In this respect, solidarity with Eastern Europe is crucial to the credibility of Western Europe's commitment to its own principles, to its own independence, to its own identity.

But how can this solidarity be made effective, without jeopardising the common interest in détente and cooperation? More specifically, what link can be established between the economic and technological contacts which the Soviet Union wants and the human ones which it is reluctant to accept?

To link or not to link

This is the famous problem of 'linkage' popularised by the Jackson amendment in the USA (linking emigration with the granting of the most Favoured nation status and of credits to communist countries) and, in Europe, by the so-called 'Third Basket' of the CSCE consisting in 'human and other contacts', including culture, education and information. Probably the most tangible (if not the only) achievement of détente resulting from Western initiative rather than from the acceptance of Soviet claims and positions lies in the reluctant acceptance by the latter, of contacts between societies and individuals as a matter of international concern and negotiation. But the limits and difficulties, due to the vigilance and rigidity of the *Abgrenzung* policy, practised by communist régimes, have usually been even more apparent and shown the fragility of every strategy adopted in this respect by the various Western Ostpolitiks.

138

One can distinguish three possible strategies, of which only the first, perhaps, really deserves the name. It consists in bargaining technology against culture (as suggested, for instance, by Peter Wiles), computers against newspapers, the circulation of goods against the circulation of people and ideas. This is what was done by the Jackson Amendment (trade against emigration) and, to some extent, by the European states at the CSCE (Basket I, on security, and II, on economic cooperation, against Basket III).

The limits of this strategy are difficult to know in advance, but they are likely to be reached fairly soon. On the Eastern side, Soviet régimes are not likely to accept fundamental modifications which could create risks for their authority, especially at a time when their economic bargaining power has improved. Conversely, on the Western side, private enterprises, especially multinational corporations in search of profits and governments in search of security and détente, are not likely to consistently subordinate these interests to the cause of human rights or communication. Finally, if it is to be applied with any success, the strategy must mobilise a bargaining power which only the USA and, to a much lesser extent, the Federal Republic can possess, but not the other European states or the Community as such.

The second strategy relies on the actual or anticipated failure of the first: it consists in putting the Soviet and East European refusal to bargain to tactical or polemical use. The goal may be to reject unpleasant Eastern demands or to rally the support of Western public opinion against unconditional détente.

This has often been used by Western diplomacy, to delay or block negotiations like the CSCE. It may be at the back of the mind of many promoters of the Jackson Amendment who may be more interested in shattering illusions about détente than in improving the fate of Soviet and East European populations. It often means an admission of failure disguised with a certain cynicism behind an expression of concern. It is often legitimate as a diplomatic or propaganda device, but consists more in the use of Ostpolitik themes for West European defensive interests than in an Ostpolitik as such.

The third strategy also stems from scepticism about the feasibility of the first. It consists, in fact, in replacing any direct strategy by an act of faith, trusting the long range process of détente. In its most general, optimistic and dogmatic form, it relies on the belief that trade brings peace and prosperity brings freedom. The link does not have to be established through bargaining since it already exists through an automatic mechanism.

In various more realistic, more subtle or more activistic versions, formulated by Willy Brandt or by Henry Kissinger, the idea is to use the process for influencing the behaviour of the ruling élite in communist countries. The rationale of Ostpolitik is that greater self-confidence and stability in the East, especially in the GDR, should lead to greater relaxation and a greater acceptance of dialogue and communication; one rationale of Kissinger's version of détente is that involving the Soviet Union in cooperative enterprises will give a number of individuals, factions or organisations a stake in détente which will influence the behaviour of the Soviet government in case of crisis.

None of the more sophisticated proponents of the 'process approach' would claim any certainty, nor even any high confidence, that it will work. Their argument would be that there is no alternative and that nothing is lost by trying since trade and détente are good by themselves even if they do not produce the desired evolution in the communist countries.

By and large, the argument seems valid, with a few caveats. One obviously has to combine the three approaches, with an emphasis upon the third. The first approach seen as a global bargain, constantly renewed, is unrealistic. The second has its uses but should not be made predominant or exclusive, since it would mean giving up any positive attempt at using the general desire for détente and cooperation with the East for positive goals. It is inevitable, for such a positive use, to rely on the third approach even though there is no guarantee that it will work, even in the long run, and even though both the warnings of dissidents and whatever fragmentary evidence we already have tell us that, in the short run, détente rather produces increased control, repression, centralisation and integration in the Soviet sphere.

This, precisely, is the point of the caveats. While there is no alternative to relying upon the process, a passive reliance would only mean leaving the Soviet Union free to use it in order to shore up her control in the East and to further her influence in the West. The first and second approaches, while impractical and negative if allowed to define a general policy, must be used in the management of the process of détente and cooperation, of interdependence and interpenetration, to promote at least some broad elements of reciprocity and balance. At the very least, it is up to the West to try to direct and protect the long range process. This means trying to prevent its benefits from being monopolised by the Soviet Union as against Eastern Europe and by communist states as against their societies. Conversely, it means — while direct pressures and explicit bargains can only be the exception — making it clear that while peace and trade are common interests, any intimate institutional long range cooperation implies a degree of trust which can only be jeopardised by certain types of Soviet behaviour, especially if repression is brought about by the process of cooperation itself. A certain constant, low-key leverage within a generally positive orientation, coupled with a willingness to exert pressure or resist Soviet demands in some exceptional but crucial cases, is both possible and desirable. But among nine free countries with capitalist economies and pressing domestic problems, it requires a degree of coordination which is one of the most difficult challenges to the Community.

A further reason for pessimism is that the present economic, social and political crisis of Western, and particularly European societies, increases the difficulty of the challenge even more but diminishes its degree of priority or of urgency. With the possible but only partial exception of Germany, the Nine and the Community itself have more immediate and dramatic tasks than the political steering of their relations with Eastern Europe. The effects of the crisis — particularly those of the price of oil and its effects on balances of payments — seem to encourage the primacy of the superpowers (whose relations more than ever constitute the framework of any Ostpolitik), a differentiation between national situations within the Community (especially between the Federal Republic and its partners, particularly Britain and Italy) and a more general integration, or at least interdependence, of Western industrial countries, including the USA and Japan and, in some respects of the whole planetary system. This includes the Communist countries and the Third World, which are confronted with problems — like famine or energy — which can no longer be solved by any particular group of countries alone.

This mixture of differentiation and interdependence makes any coherent policy of one regional group towards another exceedingly difficult. But on the other hand, while the salience and the scope of any Ostpolitik as such are reduced, new problems emerge which may reintroduce East—West relations indirectly, or through the back door.

We have already mentioned the economic aspect, which inspires a new type of Ostpolitik: Helmut Schmidt and Valéry Giscard d'Estaing may have less faith in the political de-Stalinisation or de-satellisation of Eastern Europe than Willy Brandt or Charles de Gaulle, but they do take a more active interest in Ostpolitik than expected because they have a new belief in its economic advantages.

Diplomatically, the problems of the Middle East, of Cyprus and of the Balkans have both an important East—West dimension and a direct relevance for Western Europe. Whether in relations with Greece or with

Portugal, the diplomacy of the Nine and the attraction of the Common Market have a limited but real role in avoiding polarisation along American versus Soviet lines. The possible crisis over the future of Yugoslavia after Tito may raise even more direct and certainly more dramatic issues which may put into question the very future of détente. The encouragement of links with the Common Market and of a common language between the Nine and the small, neutral and non-aligned countries of Europe, such as emerged in the CSCE on a number of issues, may play a part in preventing such a crisis.

But these are partial aspects of a more general problem, which one could call the mutual influence of domestic crises in a period of instability. This instability seems to be touching the whole Mediterranean area, from Yugoslavia to Portugal, including Greece, Turkey, Italy and Spain. The general trend seems to be towards radicalisation or 'Third-Worldisation', with the possibility of communist participation and preventive or subsequent right-wing or American reaction. These developments may threaten both détente and the European balance. Again the role of the Community may be to provide a Western presence, framework or link which, by not being strictly Atlanticist, may contribute to preventing this polarisation.

But the Community itself may be affected. One of the most important trends in Europe, encouraged but not created by the economic crisis, is the possibility of the left winning power in France, Italy and Spain, with communist participation or domination. It seems that the Soviet Union and the communist parties are extremely cautious about these perspectives, precisely because they fear domestic confrontations which may favour fascist takeovers, and international consequences which may favour forces hostile to détente in the two crucial countries — like a Jackson administration in the USA or a Strauss one in the Federal Republic. But they certainly ask for an implicit or explicit price, in foreign policy, from Henry Kissinger or Valéry Giscard d'Estaing, for their moderating influence on Western Communist parties. The East—West dimension is thus introduced, more than it ever was, into the domestic politics of Western Europe, with disturbing implications for Ostpolitik, if the preferred solution is to be a stricter division into spheres of influence based on the principle of *'cujus regio ejus religio'*. The role of Western Europe should be to prevent both polarisation within the Community or its respective countries and a rigid homogenisation or *Gleichschaltung* along Cold War lines. The problem raised is the degree of homogeneity required for the smooth functioning of regional organisations and the influence of their mutual relations upon this inner diversity or homogeneity.

The goal, in this respect, is to introduce some of the Western tolerance for diversity into Eastern Europe rather than some of the East's established homogeneity into Western Europe.

Europe today is divided at least along three lines. The classical East—West line is still the most important. But the vertical division between the two superpowers and the small and middle powers, and the socio-economic one between a rich and relatively stable North and a poor and agitated South are increasingly relevant. Along all three dimensions the role of the Community is to try to build bridges and to reduce gaps in order to provide both a more balanced structure of power and a more genuine and reciprocal structure of dialogue. Seen in this light, the Community, whatever its other concerns, can never evade the necessity of having an Ostpolitik.

Notes

1 Cf. J.F. Brown, 'Détente and Soviet Policy in Eastern Europe', *Survey*, Spring/Summer 1974, p. 46—58.

Index

Glossary

ACE	Allied Command Europe Mobile Force
ADM	Atomic Demolition Mines
CENTAG	Central Army Group
CMEA	Council for Mutual Economic Assistance (cf. Comecon)
COMECON	Cf. the above
CSCE	Conference on Security and Cooperation in Europe
ECE	Economic Commission for Europe
ECSC	European Coal and Steel Community
EDC	European Defence Community
EEC	European Economic Community
EURATOM	European Atomic Community
FRG	Federal Republic of Germany
GDR	German Democratic Republic
MBFR	Mutual Balanced Force Reduction
MC	Military Committee (NATO)
MFR	Mutual Force Reduction
M/IRBM	Medium/Intermediate Range Ballistic Missile
MIRV	Multiple Independently targetable Re-entry Vehicle
MRBM	Medium Range Ballistic Missile
NATO	North Atlantic Treaty Organisation
NDAC	Nuclear Affairs Defence Committee
NPG	Nuclear Planning Group
NORTHAG	Northern Army Group
OECD	Organisation for Economic Cooperation and Development
OEEC	Organisation for European Economic Cooperation
PGM	Precision Guided Munitions
SACEUR	Supreme Allied Commander Europe
SALT	Strategic Arms Limitation Talks
ULMS	Underwater Long Range Missile System
USAFE	United States Air Forces Europe
USNANEUR	United States Naval Forces Europe
WEU	Western European Union
WTO	Warsaw Treaty Organisation

The Author

Ieuan John was educated at the University College of South Wales, Cardiff and the London School of Economics and has lectured in International Politics at the University College of Wales, Aberystwyth since 1947.

He was appointed Woodrow Wilson Professor and Head of the Department in November 1974.

Soc
HC
241.25
E35
J6